Becoming
Legal

Immigration Law
and Mixed-Status Families

RUTH GOMBERG-MUÑOZ

New York   Oxford
OXFORD UNIVERSITY PRESS

Oxford University Press is a department of the University of Oxford.
It furthers the University's objective of excellence in research,
scholarship, and education by publishing worldwide.

Oxford   New York
Auckland   Cape Town   Dar es Salaam   Hong Kong   Karachi
Kuala Lumpur   Madrid   Melbourne   Mexico City   Nairobi
New Delhi   Shanghai   Taipei   Toronto

With offices in
Argentina   Austria   Brazil   Chile   Czech Republic   France   Greece
Guatemala   Hungary   Italy   Japan   Poland   Portugal   Singapore
South Korea   Switzerland   Thailand   Turkey   Ukraine   Vietnam

For titles covered by Section 112 of the US Higher Education
Opportunity Act, please visit www.oup.com/us/he for the
latest information about pricing and alternate formats.

Published by Oxford University Press
198 Madison Avenue, New York, New York 10016
http://www.oup.com

Oxford is a registered trademark of Oxford University Press

Library of Congress Cataloging-in-Publication Data
Names: Gomberg-Muñoz, Ruth.
Title: Becoming legal : immigration law and mixed status families / Ruth
    Gomberg-Muñoz.
Description: New York : Oxford University Press, 2016. | Includes
    bibliographical references and index.
Identifiers: LCCN 2016004806 | ISBN 9780190276010 (paperback)
Subjects: LCSH: United States--Emigration and immigration--Social aspects. |
    Immigrant families--United States--Social conditions. | Immigrant families--
    Legal status, laws, etc.--United States. | Emigration and immigration law--
    Social aspects--United States. | United States--Emigration and immigration--
    Government policy. | BISAC: SOCIAL SCIENCE / Anthropology /
    General. | SOCIAL SCIENCE / Anthropology / Cultural. | SOCIAL SCIENCE /
    Ethnic Studies / Hispanic American Studies.
Classification: LCC JV6475 .G65 2016 | DDC 305.9/069120973--dc23 LC record
    available at https://lccn.loc.gov/2016004806

Printing number: 9 8 7 6 5 4 3 2 1

Printed in the United States of America
on acid-free paper

CONTENTS

iii

....

"Why don't you become legal?"
In the midst of my fieldwork for this project, the undocumented journalist José Antonio Vargas wrote a cover story for *Time Magazine* about his experiences traveling across the United States and talking to people about his status. In his essay, Vargas addresses several questions that people often ask him about being undocumented. The question that Vargas says frustrates him most is, "Why don't you become legal?" In his story, Vargas explains that there is no path to lawful status for people like him, and a flowchart accompanying the article illustrates just how long and obstructed pathways to U.S. immigration can be. There are only two relatively quick and sure-fire routes to lawful immigration depicted on the flowchart. One is for people who are "extraordinarily accomplished or wealthy investors," and the other is for spouses, parents, and minor children of U.S. citizens (Vargas 2012).

Narrow as they are, even those pathways to legal immigration are not for undocumented people like Vargas; they are reserved for people who are legally present or have never been to the United States at all. For people like Vargas, being undocumented further complicates an already difficult journey to lawful U.S. immigration.

"Why don't they become legal?" It is a question that I, too, have been asked many times. Sometimes the question is phrased, "Why don't they come legally?" but the assumption is the same: there are legal avenues to U.S. immigration, so why don't undocumented people use them? The first time I was asked this question, I was teaching a course as a graduate student at the University of Illinois at Chicago. "But, why don't they just come legally?" one student asked about undocumented Mexican workers. I was foolishly taken aback. "They have a better chance at winning the lottery than migrating legally," I replied, sure of the answer even as I realized that I had no idea why. The United States admits more legal immigrants annually than any other country on the globe. If the U.S. immigration system is so generous, why do millions of people enter and stay unlawfully? This question, as well as the fact that I did not quite know the answer, bothered me for years. It was not until I wrote this book that I began to understand how difficult it is for certain people to migrate legally and to change their status once they are undocumented.

On the day that Vargas's *Time* issue hit the stands, I was in Evanston, Illinois, having coffee with a young woman I call Anya. We were discussing Anya and her husband Enrique's attempt to change his immigration status—an attempt that was ultimately successful but left them separated for months, thousands of dollars in debt, and deeply disillusioned with the U.S. immigration system. "Did you hear about this?" I asked her, showing her a picture of the just-released magazine on my phone. She had not, but we were both eager to read it. When I left Anya's home, I went to the nearest bookstore and bought five copies of the magazine, and then I sat in my car and flipped through it. I stopped when I got to the flowchart and called Anya. "The story is nice," I said, "But you won't believe this chart," and I described the flowchart with its two short lines. "Oh, no," Anya groaned, "now people will be more confused than ever."

*   *   *

There is a common perception in the United States that marriage to a U.S. citizen puts hopeful immigrants on a quick and easy path to lawful U.S. residency. In 2009, the highest grossing romantic comedy in the United States was a movie called *The Proposal*. In the film, the lead character, played by Sandra Bullock, forces an employee into marriage so that she can avoid deportation to Canada. (Readers of my generation may remember a similar movie, *Green Card*, which was released in 1990.) For Bullock's character, a wealthy Canadian executive who entered the United States with a work visa, such a ploy might just work.

The U.S. immigration system is designed to prioritize family reunification, and two-thirds of U.S. immigrant visas issued each year are granted to family members of U.S. citizens and lawful residents (McKay 2003). Marriage to a U.S. citizen moves prospective immigrants into the top priority category for immigration, where they become immediately eligible to apply for a U.S. immigrant visa, or green card.

But for people who have entered the United States unlawfully and live here without papers, the pathway to lawful status is neither short nor easy, even for those with U.S.-citizen spouses. This is because two parts of the U.S. immigration system collide when they try to become legal. One part makes them eligible for a family-based visa, but requires them to leave the United States to get it. Another part then blocks them from returning for 10 years. Only select applicants whose U.S.-citizen petitioner can prove he or she would suffer "extreme hardship" in the event of a 10-year separation will be allowed to return. In essence, the "legal nonexistence" (Coutin 2000a) of undocumented people reroutes them into a program, consular processing, which is designed for family members of U.S. citizens awaiting their visas abroad, in their countries of origin. And, as a result, an immigration system that purports to prioritize family unification tears mixed-status families apart.

This book follows members of mixed-status families as they navigate the long and bumpy road of U.S. immigration processing. I explore how families negotiate each step along the way, from the decision to undertake legalization, to the interview at the U.S. consulate in Ciudad Juárez, Mexico, to the effort to put together a case of extreme hardship so that the undocumented family member can return. I also discuss families' efforts to rebuild their lives in the aftermath of immigration processing—both for those who are successful and for those who are not. At every juncture, I highlight how standards for U.S. immigration processing compel families to conform to normative prototypes of family, morality, and need—each one undergirded by racial, gendered, and class-based foundations. As families understand and take on those standards, they reveal both the power of U.S. immigration law and the limits of its reach in their everyday lives.

ACKNOWLEDGMENTS

O ver the course of four years, I interviewed some 60 people who shared stories of their experiences with the U.S. immigration system. I talked with many of them several times; they invited me into their homes and introduced me to their partners and children. With some, I established friendships that I hope to sustain for the long term. Others have been effectively severed from my society, forced to leave the United States because they or their loved one can no longer live here. To all of you, I am deeply grateful for the contribution your story made to this book. I hope the book honors your truths and does justice to your struggles to keep your families together.

I am also indebted to several immigration policy experts—both professional and lay—including José Manuel Ventura, Anna Katz Piñera, Rachel Campero, Rachel Prado, Chad Doobay, and Diego Bonesatti, for patiently walking me through the vagaries of immigration processing time and again. The errors that remain—and there will be errors, despite their best efforts and my own—are my fault alone. I am also grateful to Sarah Horton for reading the manuscript and providing thoughtful criticism on every chapter. I thank Susan Bibler Coutin, who read an early draft of the book's central argument and provided critical insights on it, and Ana Croegaert, who pushed me to develop a gendered analysis of immigration processing. I am also grateful for the friendship and guidance of Chicago-area colleagues who specialize in migration. In particular, Rosa Cabrera, Molly Doane, Nilda Flores Gonzalez, Vanessa Guridy Cerritos, Almita Miranda,

Amalia Pallares, and Alaka Wali provided useful insights for this project. Colleagues further afield, including Josiah Heyman and Tanya Golash-Boza, also offered guidance and support on this work. This project was funded by the National Science Foundation (NSF) under Grant 1233022. I am tremendously grateful to the NSF for funding this research, and I thank all of the anonymous reviewers who vetted my proposal and helped strengthen the project before it got off the ground. I especially thank the program director, Deborah Winslow, who helped me through the revision process with patience and expertise. NSF funding made it possible for me to have two excellent graduate assistants. Laura Nussbaum-Barberena assisted me in the early stages of data collection and was especially helpful in making contacts with immigration-oriented legal offices in Chicago. Later, Diana Guelespe helped develop components of this research into related applied projects; these count among my most rewarding work to date.

Sherith Pankratz at Oxford University Press is everything an editor should be: she is passionate, knowledgeable, and encouraging; I am so grateful for her support of this project. Meredith Keffer, her assistant editor, has tremendous talent and an infectious love of social science that bodes well for her scholarly career. Thanks and turtles to both of you. I also thank the following reviewers for their thoughtful and incisive comments on the manuscript: Lori Brown, Meredith College; Leo R. Chavez, University of California, Irvine; Luz María Gordillo, Washington State University, Vancouver; Sarah Horton, University of Colorado, Denver; Cecilia Menjívar, Arizona State University; Enrique C. Ochoa, California State University, Los Angeles; Anna Ochoa O'Leary, University of Arizona; Jacqueline Stevens, Northwestern University; and one anonymous reviewer. Portions of Chapter 6 were previously published in: Gomberg-Muñoz, Ruth. 2016. The Juárez Wives Club: Gendered citizenship and US immigration law. *American Ethnologist* 43(2). Portions of Chapter 5 were previously published in: Gomberg-Muñoz, Ruth. 2015. The Punishment/ El Castigo: Undocumented Latinos and US Immigration Processing. *Journal of Ethnic and Migration Studies* 41(14): 2235–2252. I thank the editors and reviewers at *American Ethnologist* and the *Journal of Ethnic and Migration Studies* for their helpful critiques of those manuscripts.

The anthropology faculty at Loyola University Chicago, my academic home, has welcomed me with warmth and collegiality. I am grateful to Kristin Krueger for her friendship and to Kathleen Adams and Ben Penglase for productive, engaging hallway discussions about anthropological theory, teaching and learning, and the everyday ethics of ethnographic research.

I also thank Anne Grauer, Flip Arnold, Jim Calcagno, Dan Amick, Thea Strand, Juliet Brophy, Catherine Nichols, and Noah Butler for making academia a pleasure, as well as Patty Robertson, our department administrator, for keeping me on the right side of Loyola's administrative offices. I am also appreciative of the students at the University of Illinois at Chicago and Loyola, too numerous to name, who have challenged me to think sharply, write clearly, and do more. The future is in good hands with you.

For many years, my work in and outside academia has been inspired and enriched by undocumented activists, friends, and family members. Most remain "in the shadows," and I am unable to publish their names. Of those who are "out," I especially thank Jorge Mena, Reyna Wences, Rigo Padilla, Ireri Unzueta Carrasco, and Martin Unzueta for their willingness to help me with my research, teaching, and thinking.

My very own family deserves special thanks for making this book possible. My father, Paul Gomberg, is a political philosopher and antiracist activist who has patiently and critically guided my academic work and shaped my thinking for a lifetime. His influence is on every page. My mother, Mary Conklin Gomberg, is not a copy editor, but she could be; I thank her for reading my work carefully and critically and for making incisive suggestions and correcting many of my writing errors. I am also grateful for my adoptive families, the Pérezes, Muñozes, O'Connors, and O'Reillys, who are a constant source of warmth and support, and for April McCraw Lancaster, who has been teaching me about friendship for most of my life. It really does take a village to raise a child, especially when you are simultaneously trying to write a book, and I am indebted to the core women of my village: Mary Gomberg, Jane Dickman, Caitlyn Solomon, Simone Johnson, and Christine Cupicciotti, who cared for my child while I worked. My partner, Manuel Muñoz, continuously moves my thinking and writing forward through long discussions about the politics of everyday life. His willingness to be an active and involved co-parent makes my life inside and outside academia possible. Thank you, Manuel.

Finally, I thank my son, Isaac. I received word that the NSF was going to fund this research project a mere six days after Isaac was born. Once the panic subsided, I struggled to do right by both of my babies, Isaac and the research, during the ensuing months and years. Isaac did what he could to help: he cried during interviews, woke me up at 4:00 am as often as possible, and, as he grew, firmly insisted that I stop working for playtime. Having Isaac may not have made my research easier in the end, but it taught me more about love and family than anything else in the world. For that, I am most grateful of all.

LEGALIZATION FLOWCHART

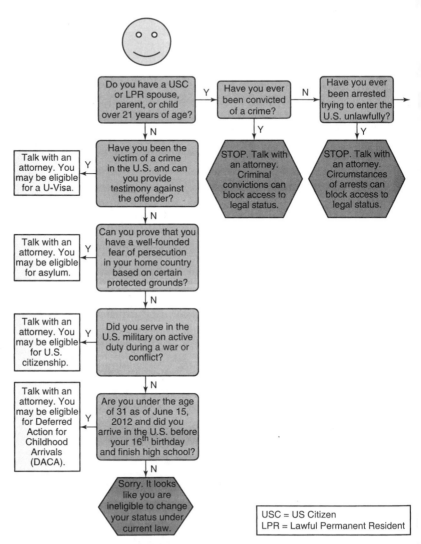

UNDOCUMENTED AND HOPING TO CHANGE YOUR STATUS? See whether you qualify under current U.S. law.

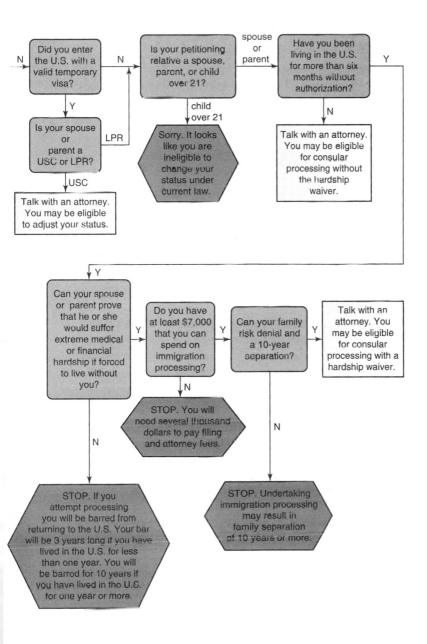

For Mary and Paul Gomberg

CHAPTER 1

Four Million Families

René and Molly

René likes fireworks. He is especially proud of his 4th of July fireworks show, which draws dozens of family members, friends, and neighbors to his annual backyard barbecue. The sale of exploding fireworks is banned in his home state of Illinois, so René buys them just across the state line in Indiana. His wife, Molly, drives, since René does not have a driver's license. This year, René's fireworks are especially good, and this worries me a little. The night before, the local news had reported that Chicago police would be cracking down on illegal fireworks, even arresting people who set them off. But René and Molly are not worried, and there are at least two police officers in attendance at the barbecue, so I try to relax and enjoy the show. I watch as my young son waves a glow stick around in delight.

René is doing what many U.S. citizens do on the 4th of July: grilling hot dogs and hamburgers, drinking beer, and setting off fireworks. His three children and their friends are alternately jumping around on the trampoline and into the swimming pool. His family and friends are sitting at patio tables, eating potato chips, drinking beer, and discussing U.S. gun laws. A bit drunk, they sing "God Bless America" as the fireworks climax. It is a quintessential American scene. Only René is not a U.S. citizen; whether he can be considered an American mostly depends on your perspective.

When René came to the United States from Mexico 20 years ago, he did not plan to stay. Like most undocumented people in the United States, he thought he would work for a few years, save some money, and return home. He did go back to Mexico once, to see his parents. He was caught on the U.S.–Mexico border as he came back to Chicago, and that trip sabotaged his chances of legalizing his immigration status—although he did not know it at the time. Because René is undocumented, the little risks that he takes, like driving without a license and setting off illicit fireworks, can have serious consequences. In ever-increasing numbers, undocumented immigrants are being deported from the United States following arrests for these kinds of minor infractions.

Despite the risks, René stays. Where else would he go? His wife and three children are U.S. citizens; they are from Chicago and uninterested in relocating to Mexico. René's long-time job is in Chicago, and his house is in Chicago; most of his friends are in Chicago now, too. As he flips burgers on the grill, René's Chicago Bears tattoo peeks out from under his shirtsleeve. In most meaningful ways, René's home, his only home now, is Chicago. That is why he and Molly still hope to change his immigration status someday: they want to stay together, and they want to stay here.

In some ways, René fits the stereotypical image of an undocumented immigrant. He is from Mexico, and he came to the United States as a young man in search of work. He lived, worked, and made his way around those first few years mostly in the company of other young Mexican men. He works in a restaurant as a busboy; his pay is just less than the U.S. average, and he has little hope for advancement here.

In other ways, René defies most popular stereotypes of undocumented people. He has lived in the United States for two decades, is married to a U.S. citizen, speaks English fluently, owns his own home, and is deeply integrated into U.S. society. These unexpected parts of René's story are more common than you might imagine, and they are getting more so every day.

In the early 1990s, I worked in a restaurant with several undocumented Mexican workers. Although they had been working in the United States for years, these men were more or less active migrants who would return to their homes in Zacatecas, Mexico, once a year. Those visits cost them approximately $200 each time; sometimes they would get caught at the border, and then they would immediately try to cross again. The risks were small, and the payoff—getting to visit family in Mexico and return to work in Chicago—was worth it.

That migration experience is unrecognizable for those who traverse the U.S.–Mexico border today. Now, the U.S.–Mexico border is fortified with miles of steel fencing, high-tech detection systems, and tens of thousands of Border Patrol agents equipped with trucks, dogs, drones, global positioning systems, and light aircraft (Chacon and Davis 2006; Meyers 2005). Perhaps paradoxically, militarized efforts to "defend" the border have made it far more dangerous. The effects on migrants are relentless and deadly serious: people now die crossing the U.S.–Mexico border at a rate of nearly one every day (U.S. Customs and Border Protection 2014); theft, rape, kidnapping, and assault are ubiquitous; the consequences of getting caught migrating increasingly include federal criminal prosecution and a prison sentence prior to deportation; and the cost has swelled to anywhere between $1,000 and $10,000 per person per trip.

Much as a perilous U.S.–Mexico border makes it more difficult for some undocumented people to enter the United States, it also makes it more difficult for them to leave. Rather than risk leaving and being unable to come back, more and more undocumented people stay where they are. Thus, one consequence of border militarization has been an increase in the number of undocumented people who settle in the United States for the long term. As of 2010, two-thirds of the undocumented population had been living in the United States for 10 years or more (Taylor et al. 2011). For migrants like my friends from Zacatecas, border militarization and settlement mean prolonged and indefinite separation from their family members in Mexico (see Abrego 2014; Boehm 2012); for people like René, they also mean ever-lengthening ties with family and community within the United States.

In the past, undocumented people who lived in the United States for long periods and could demonstrate close family ties to U.S. citizens were able to legalize their immigration status. Policy changes in the 1990s and early 2000s have now made it nearly impossible for millions of people to do so, regardless of their family ties or length of residence. Between border policies that hem them in and immigration policies that keep them "illegal," there are more undocumented people living in the United States as members of mixed-status families—families that have undocumented, legally resident, and/or U.S.-citizen members—than ever before. In total, there are some 16.6 million people in the United States in families with at least one undocumented member (Taylor et al. 2011); if we assume a family average of 3.5 people, that means that the United States is home to more than 4 million mixed-status families.

Every year, more than 20,000 undocumented people in mixed-status families apply to legalize their status through consular processing (U.S. Department of Homeland Security 2013). Consular processing is the only family-based pathway to legal status for people who have entered the country without permission, and it requires the undocumented person to leave the United States and go to the U.S. consulate in their country of origin. When they do, all but a few trigger a 10-year bar on their return. Some undocumented people can have the bar waived if their U.S.-citizen relative can show that he or she would suffer "extreme hardship" in the event of a 10-year separation or relocation. If the bar is waived, the undocumented person can reenter the United States as a legal immigrant. Only undocumented people who have a U.S.-citizen or lawfully resident spouse or parent are eligible for a waiver of the 10-year bar, and those lucky few face a gauntlet of onerous criteria, complicated forms, expensive fees, and indefinite separation to reach—if their luck holds—lawful permanent U.S. residency at the end.

As they undertake this process, families confront onerous criteria for inclusion with lives that are already meaningfully included, and they must distort, degrade, and even jeopardize their relationships to stay together. Their experiences with consular processing reveal oft-hidden arenas of political contradiction, in which policies designed to reunite families force them apart, people deemed unworthy of U.S. citizenship are transformed into potential U.S. citizens, and policies that boost the value of U.S. citizenship degrade U.S. citizens in practice. Together, they illuminate moments when legal exclusion and lived inclusion collide, bringing nuances and ambiguities of power into sharper focus. That process is the subject of this book.

The Argument

In anthropology, the lives of transnational migrants are often described as being divided. They are "neither here nor there" (Striffler 2007; Zavella 2011) or "half here, half there" (Boehm 2012), "in between" (Schuck 1998), or "in both places" (Gomberg-Muñoz 2011). For undocumented people, the social and physical displacement of migration is compounded by political exclusion and marginality. Undocumented people are characterized as "impossible subjects" (Ngai 2004) and "alien citizens" (Bosniak 2006) who live "in the shadows" (Chavez 1992) of "spaces of nonexistence" (Coutin 2000a), where they are "abjected" (Gonzales and Chavez 2012; Willen 2007) by the state and reduced to a condition of "bare life" (De Genova 2010) and even "social death" (Cacho 2012). This literature provides scholars of migration with a common language to discuss the experiences of unauthorized migrants who originate from and settle in disparate places, and it has made a vital contribution to our understanding of how nationalist policies in the context of globalization can create new and pernicious forms of inequality. In particular, recent ethnographies have examined how punitive immigration policies divide families across borders, revealing their effects on those who move and on those they leave behind (Abrego 2014; Boehm 2012; Zavella 2011). Here I shift the focus to families that are not divided by borders but are differentiated by status (see also Dreby 2015), complementing this scholarship with a look at how mixed-status families undertake immigration processing to stay safely together and, in the process, oppose their division and exclusion.

With this book, I contribute two arguments to the scholarship on unauthorized migration. First, I show how undocumented status is experienced neither uniformly nor in isolation from other structures of political and socioeconomic inequality. Instead, undocumented people experience uneven measures of marginalization and belonging that are shaped by long-standing racial, class, sexual, and gendered U.S. inequalities. I describe how these inequalities make it more difficult for some undocumented people to legalize their immigration status than others and how they continue to shape the opportunities of newly legal immigrants. I focus especially on growing linkages between U.S. immigration and criminal justice systems, and I argue that these systems both reproduce racial and class inequalities and mask them with putatively race-neutral standards.

Second, I show how undocumented people and their U.S.-citizen family members forge connections across sociopolitical categories, as people who hold different statuses share in each other's lives. These connections pose a challenge to state policies that seek to neatly divide people into those who belong and those who do not, and they expose the incongruity that results when discrete categories are superimposed onto complex and intertwined lives. This incongruity comes into especially sharp focus when couples undertake immigration processing and U.S. citizens find themselves at the center of immigration petitions. There, they learn that their citizenship offers little protection from stigmatization, bureaucratic indifference, financial ruin, and vulnerability to prolonged family separation. In this process, immigration policies both uphold the value of U.S. citizenship in theory and degrade U.S. citizens in practice.

Together, these points highlight both distinctions within citizenship statuses and linkages between citizens and noncitizens, offering balance to the recent trend in migration scholarship that has emphasized the capacity of state policies to enact distinctions between "legal" and "nonlegal" people. Here, I seek to complement that scholarship with a reminder that immigration policies are never absolute or unidirectional but always interactive and contested "from below;" moreover, lives are never "bare" for those who live them, but always interconnected, meaningful, and complex.

For general readers and students, I hope that this book provides useful insights into U.S. immigration processing and the ways in which immigration policies affect undocumented people, lawful immigrants, and U.S. citizens alike. I also hope that this book helps readers more fully understand central questions in U.S. immigration debates, such as: Why don't undocumented people wait their turn to enter the United States legally? And, why don't they legalize their status once they have U.S.-citizen relatives? More broadly, I hope that this book augments readers' understandings of unauthorized migration with a look at how undocumented people are embedded in the same familial ties that envelope all of us and give meaning to our lives as sons and daughters, parents and partners, and siblings and friends.

As scholars, we always tell one part of a bigger story. The story that I focus on here is not about border crossings, but about how people try to build a stable life where they are. And it is not a story of family separation or conflict per se, but of family members' struggles to stay together. A focus on agency, attachment, and commitment in a time of record-breaking deportation requires a tricky balancing act that neither minimizes the perils of illegal status nor underestimates the strength of human resiliency and connection. Although I focus on how families navigate immigration processing mostly voluntarily, I urge readers to keep in mind that their struggles take place as part of a broader system of forcible detention, deportation, and dehumanization that ensnares hundreds of thousands of U.S. immigrants every year.

The Project

This book presents results from a multiyear ethnographic project that explored how people undertake U.S. immigration processing and live in its aftermath. In many ways, this project is a continuation of a previous study, in which I examined how undocumented workers in Chicago, including René, develop strategies to enhance their stability and well-being in light of their immigration status. Not surprisingly, my participants in that study lamented the constraints that undocumented status placed on their upward mobility and long-term security in the United States. In the months following the completion of that project, I became especially interested in how undocumented people's lives change when they become "legal" and, just as important, how their lives stay the same. That interest gave rise to this project.

When I put together a proposal to do an ethnographic study of people undertaking immigration processing, I was sure that I had the social connections to complete the research. After all, I began working in restaurants with undocumented people 20 years ago, and I have been active, on and off, in Chicago's immigrant rights movement ever since. Today, I continue to work with undocumented people on a daily basis, and I live as part of a mixed-status community.

But as I set out to recruit ethnographic participants in the spring of 2011, I quickly became stymied. I know many people who are undocumented, but almost none of them can change his or her status. So I started the project by interviewing undocumented people who wanted to change their status and had at least looked into it, regardless of whether they were ultimately eligible to legalize. I recruited 17 people in that category and interviewed them in the summers of 2011, 2012, and 2013. By the end of my three-year field season, none of them had been able to get lawful U.S. residency. Three were granted Deferred Action for Childhood Arrivals (DACA), 2 attained a U visa, which is a kind of conditional visa, and 1 was deported. One young woman, Lily, was put in deportation proceedings but then her case was closed; later, she applied for and received DACA. All of these study participants are of Latin American origin, and the overwhelming majority are from Mexico (Appendix A).

A few months into the research, I met Anya. Not only was Anya going through immigration processing with her husband, Enrique (Enrique was actually in Mexico for immigration processing when Anya and I met the first time), but also she was part of a support group with other mixed-status couples undertaking immigration processing. Between Anya's contacts and my own, I recruited a total of 25 people who had begun family-based processing, and I followed them over the course of the three-year field season. Eight of them adjusted their status successfully from within the United States. The remaining 17 undertook consular processing abroad; of them, 9 were ultimately successful, 7 were unsuccessful and now live either separately or outside of the United States, and 1 attained a conditional visa (Appendix B). This is a somewhat lower approval rate than the average; between 2010 and 2015, nearly 80 percent of mixed-status families who undertook consular processing were approved (Kowalski 2015).

To round out the interview portion of the research, I conducted interviews with another 17 people who are either long-term lawful residents or naturalized U.S. citizens, and I interviewed three immigration attorneys and three legal representatives accredited by the Bureau of Immigration Affairs, as well as staff members at five immigration legal clinics in Chicago.

In all, I conducted more than 100 interviews with 68 people. Most of them live in the Chicago area, and I went to see them where they live or work. I also interviewed people in other areas of the United States, including Atlanta, Indianapolis, Madison, and Washington, D.C., either after a long road trip or via Skype, phone, or email. Additionally, I interviewed 3 people who have been displaced indefinitely by immigration processing and live abroad, 2 in Mexico and 1 in Bolivia; these interviews were conducted via Skype, email, and telephone.

The U.S. Department of Homeland Security (DHS) reports that, in 2011, the U.S. Citizenship and Immigration Services (USCIS) adjudicated more than 23,000 hardship waiver petitions, about 75 percent of which, or more than 17,000, were processed in Mexico.[1] It is difficult to know whether the experiences of the mixed-status couples who I interviewed are representative of this larger population because data from the DHS do not distinguish between consulate applicants who have never resided in the United States and those who leave in an attempt to change their undocumented status. I suspect that my data are biased in that most of my undocumented participants who successfully adjusted their status were men who were petitioned by their U.S.-citizen wives. Data from the DHS indicate that nearly two-thirds of green cards for immediate relatives of U.S. citizens are issued to women; thus, undocumented women who have been petitioned by their U.S.-citizen husbands are underrepresented in my sample.

My study participants are also largely members of nuclear family units, working or middle class, embedded in mixed-status or nonimmigrant communities, and generally well informed about immigration procedures. These characteristics—belonging in a nuclear family unit, social and cultural capital, and deep ties within the United States—are not incidental to their experiences with the U.S. immigration system. As I will show, mixed-status family members strategically draw on these qualities to strengthen their immigration cases. This is ironic, since it is precisely family unity, financial stability, and belonging in the United States that immigration processing most threatens to destroy. In all, I suspect that there is enormous diversity among the families who undertake consular processing and that the ethnoracial, familial, and class characteristics of my research participants are neither anomalous nor necessarily representative of the larger population.

I took several steps to protect the privacy and confidentiality of the people who participated in this research. In particular, I changed all names and any identifying details of people and their processing experiences. In most cases, this at least involved fudging the exact dates of immigration appointments. In some instances, I worried that the specifics of a legal case could be potentially identifiable; in those cases, I "switched out" some details, attributing parts of one family's case to another family and vice versa.

I also volunteered in an immigration legal clinic during the summers of 2011, 2012, and 2013. There, I sat in on consultations, helped process DACA applications, and conducted case follow-up with the USCIS. Those experiences were valuable in helping me develop an understanding of the complexities of U.S. immigration processing, although as a matter of privacy, I do not relate any portion of client stories in this book. With permission from site administrators, I also joined an online support group for people undertaking consular processing. I call this group the Juárez Wives Club. The number of members in the group varied slightly over time, but on average there were about 600 members, with a few dozen especially active posters on the site. I used the site to gain a better understanding of prevailing questions, concerns, and advice that people have as they go through consular processing, although I do not relate any personal information or stories shared on the site here.

I also had access to important legal documents as I conducted this research. Several families were generous in letting me look at their immigration packets, which included their family petitions, visa applications, and hardship waiver petitions. I downloaded blank applications from the USCIS website to document the requirements and questions involved in immigration processing. I also read a manual entitled *A Guide for Immigration Advocates* that is published by the Immigrant Legal Resource Center. The staff attorneys at the center authored the manual and have done a wonderful job of clearly explaining the ins and outs of complex policies. Finally, this project is informed by my life as a member of an extended mixed-status family and community. For many years, I have shared the struggles of friends and loved ones as they grappled with the U.S. immigration system.

I did not start this project intending to focus on mixed-status families; my interest was in how people experience U.S. immigration processing and its outcomes. But I came to understand that, for my study participants, immigration processing is a family affair: undertaken by people as members of families and with profound effects on all family members, regardless of their immigration status. Here, I showcase the stories not only of the undocumented people who are the intended beneficiaries of immigration processing, but also of the U.S. citizens who petition for them. Although in many respects family members undertake and experience the process together, their respective contributions to and experiences with the process are shaped in different ways by citizenship status, social capital, and gender.

The Process

U.S. immigration policies that govern legalization are complicated, opaque, and generally poorly understood, even by attorneys, state agents, and immigrants themselves. Before I describe how people in mixed-status families experience U.S. immigration processing, I provide a brief introduction to the steps and approximate costs and timelines for the two main family-based programs through which undocumented people can legalize their status.[2] These programs are only open to undocumented people who have U.S. citizens or lawful residents as "immediate relatives"; undocumented people without qualifying immediate relatives are largely unable to change their status under current immigration law. Immigration programs, timelines, and costs are ever changing, and this information was current during most of the fieldwork period (2011–2013) but has changed substantially since then. I discuss some of these changes in this book, but updated information can always be found at www.uscis.gov.

Undocumented people with qualifying relatives may be eligible for one of two main family-based immigration programs. Which program they are funneled into largely depends on how they entered the United States. Those who entered on a temporary visa, such as a student or tourist visa, and overstayed it can usually adjust their status through the first program if they have a U.S. citizen spouse, parent, or child older than 21 years of age. Those who entered the United States by crossing the border unlawfully are not eligible for the first program unless they filed before April 30, 2001. Most undocumented border crossers, then, must go through the second program. As you will see, family ties and mode of entry into the United States have profound consequences for people's ability to change their immigration status.

Program One: Adjustment of Status under Section 245(a)

Adjustment of status is a procedure that allows eligible immigrants to apply to change their immigration status at a USCIS office within the United States.

Undocumented people who meet two criteria can adjust their status under this program. First, they must have an approved family visa petition through a U.S.-citizen spouse, parent, or child older than 21, and second, they must be able to show that they entered the United States lawfully, typically with a temporary visa. Undocumented people who entered the United States unlawfully are not eligible for this program.

Steps to Legalization through 245(a) Adjustment

Step	Processing Time	Approximate Cost (in U.S. dollars; includes filing and attorney fees)	Location
1. Family petition (I 130)	3–6 months (concurrent with I-485)	$1,000	United States
2. Form I-485	1 year or less	$2,000	United States
3. Biometrics	1–2 hours	$80	United States
4. Interview	1 hour	0	United States
Total	<1 year	$3,080	
Total time outside the United States: None			

Program Two: Consular Processing

Consular processing is a procedure that allows people to apply for lawful permanent residency at a U.S. consulate outside of the United States. Undocumented people who entered the United States unlawfully can go through consular processing if they have been approved for a family-based visa through a U.S.-citizen or lawfully resident spouse or parent. Those who entered with a temporary visa can also undertake consular processing if their petitioning family member is a lawful resident instead of a U.S. citizen.

Consular processing involves two main steps. The first step is for the undocumented person to leave the United States and attend an interview at the U.S. consulate in his or her home country. When they leave, all but a few are barred from returning. People who have been undocumented for between 180 days and 1 year are barred from the United States for 3 years; people who have been undocumented for 1 year or more are barred for 10 years. For both groups, consular processing involves the additional step of applying to have the bar waived, which requires a "hardship waiver" petition filed by a U.S.-citizen or lawfully resident spouse or parent.[3]

Steps to Legalization through Consular Processing
(*processing times for U.S. consulate in Ciudad Juárez, Mexico*)

Step	Processing Time	Approximate Cost (in U.S. dollars; includes travel, filing fees, and attorney costs)	Location
1. Family petition (I-130)	3–6 months	$420	United States
2. Leave the United States		>$1,000	
3. Biometrics and medical	2 days	$400	Abroad
4. Interview [barred from returning]	1 hour	0	Abroad
5. Hardship waiver (I-601)	3 weeks to 18 months or more	$7,000	Abroad
Total	**6 months to 1.5 years or more**	**>$8,820**	
Total time outside the United States: 3 weeks to permanent			

As I describe in later chapters, processing times and costs for immigration programs can vary widely and unpredictably. The families I interviewed that undertook consular processing have been separated for periods ranging from three months to several years, and the process has cost them anywhere from $7,500 to more than $30,000 in fees, attorney costs, travel, and lost income.

As arduous as the process is, many undocumented people still cannot legalize through consular processing even when they have U.S.-citizen immediate relatives. For example, René has been approved for a family-based visa because of his marriage to Molly, but their attorney has advised them not to attempt consular processing. This is because René was caught trying to reenter the United States after his most recent trip to Mexico. René and Molly have spent hundreds of dollars to track down René's immigration and criminal records, and they always come up clean. Still, their attorney advises them not to risk it. "Things come up in Juárez," she has warned them, and their application could be denied and René barred permanently from the United States. For now, René and Molly have decided to wait for a change in U.S. immigration law, and until then, René will remain undocumented.

Here, I describe consular processing as my study participants experienced it, but in March 2013, the consular processing system was changed. Instead of leaving the United States, attending an immigrant interview, and then submitting a hardship waiver application abroad, qualifying undocumented immigrants can do the waiver processing first from within the United States and then leave the United States for their consular interview. I discuss this change, called the provisional waiver program (I-601a), and its implications in more depth later, but preliminary data suggest that the new program both shortens separation times for many families and has a lower approval rate than the regular (I-601) consular processing program.

The Book

This book is organized to take readers on a journey through immigration processing, as seen from the perspective of couples who undertake it. The second chapter, "Grounds for Exclusion," lays necessary groundwork with a historical review of U.S. immigration policies. This chapter examines how normative concerns about the racial, class, gendered, and sexual characteristics of new immigrants have historically shaped U.S. immigration laws, and it follows those concerns into the current period with a description of contemporary programs for legal immigration. The following chapter, "The Family Petition," explores how mixed-status families make the decision to pursue or not to pursue consular processing. I examine how divergent immigration statuses can affect family relationships, and I describe the myriad factors that families must weigh before they make the decision to file a family petition—the first step in family-based immigration processing.

The fourth chapter, "The Punishment," follows undocumented people to the U.S. consulate in Ciudad Juárez, Mexico, as they proceed to the second step in consular processing. I describe the barrage of testing that applicants undergo, as well as the immigration consequences of each test. This chapter shows that "illegal" is not "illegal" in the same way for everyone; instead, racial, gendered, and class-based anxieties continue to underpin U.S. immigration policy and practice, making it easier for some people to pass this stage than others. The fifth chapter, "Extreme Hardship," describes the third and final stage of consular processing: the hardship waiver petition. I show how mixed-status families are compelled to distort and demean their connections to each other and the places in their lives to demonstrate legally recognized extreme hardship. I also explore how opaque and arbitrary demands of consular processing have led to the formation of the Juárez Wives Club, an online community in which members share information and compassion as they undertake immigration processing.

The sixth chapter, "Life after Legal Status," examines how families rebuild their lives when immigration processing is over. For families who are successful, I explore how newly legal status affects their ability to travel, work, and live securely; for those who are unsuccessful, I examine how they attempt to reconstruct their lives apart or abroad. The concluding chapter, "Documented and Deportable," considers contemporary trends in U.S. immigration policy. I explore some of the "fuzzy areas" of legal status (Menjívar and Kanstroom 2014) with a look at the persistent vulnerability of lawful residents and the growing number of U.S. immigrants with conditional, temporary, or provisional statuses. Finally, I advance the argument that the U.S. immigration system is a comprehensive system of inequality that benefits some while wreaking havoc on the lives of mixed-status families and the undocumented population at large.

Each chapter begins with a vignette of one family's journey through immigration processing, excerpted from my interviews and field notes. These vignettes are meant to help guide readers though processing from the perspective of families that undertake it, and each vignette also helps to illustrate the main analytical argument of the chapter. More important, these vignettes are meant to remind readers that law is never divorced from human interpretations, interactions, and experiences. Indeed, as the following chapters illustrate, members of mixed-status families experience law quite intimately, since immigration policy deeply shapes their relationships with each other and with broader U.S. society.

CHAPTER 2

Grounds for Exclusion
The U.S. Immigration System

Enrique and Anya

Enrique and Anya met in 2006, when a friend offered to set them up on a blind date. Enrique was hesitant; he had divorced from his first wife only two years earlier and was not looking for a serious relationship. But he was intrigued and maybe a little bored, and he agreed to meet Anya for dinner. Enrique found himself attracted to Anya's unguarded and self-confident personality; he also thought she was "very, very, very pretty," he laughs. He called Anya to ask her out on a second date, and they talked on the phone for more than three hours. That phone call led to another date, and then another, and soon their relationship grew more serious than either of them had expected.

When Anya and Enrique got married in 2009, they were acutely aware of two things. The first was that they would do whatever it took to legalize Enrique's immigration status; they wanted to be able to travel, have children, and live securely without the fear of deportation. They also knew that the process would be burdensome and costly. Still, although they were knowledgeable about immigration processing, determined, and organized, Anya and Enrique were little prepared for how difficult changing Enrique's immigration status would prove to be.

I met Anya in 2011, more than a year after she and Enrique had begun the process to legalize his status and nearly six months after he had left for his immigration interview in Mexico. A colleague of mine had introduced us, and

YEAR	POLICY
1790	The 1790 Naturalization Act. The U.S.'s first citizenship policy, it limits naturalization as a U.S. citizen to free white men of good moral character.
1882	Chinese Exclusion Act and Immigration Act of 1882. Suspends Chinese immigration. Levies an immigration tax of 50 cents and excludes anyone deemed a convict, lunatic, idiot, and anyone who appears "likely to become a public charge"—that is, to use welfare.
1917	The 1917 Immigration Act (Asiatic Barred Zone Act). Creates an "Asiatic barred zone" that bars the entry of people from South Asia, most of Southeast Asia, and almost all of the Middle East; keeps bars on Chinese immigration intact.
1924	The 1924 National Origins Quota Act (Johnson-Reed Act). Established numerical quotas that largely restricted immigration from areas outside of Northwest Europe.
1942	Bracero Program begins. A treaty between the United States and Mexico to import Mexican "guest" workers as temporary agricultural workers. Initially conceived as an emergency measure to respond to labor shortages during WWII, the Bracero Program lasted for 22 years.
1942	Magnuson Act. Repeals the Chinese Exclusion Act and allows Chinese to become U.S. citizens.
1952	The Immigration and Nationality Act (McCarren-Walter Act). Includes Asian nations in national-origins quota system.
1965	The 1965 Immigration and Nationality Act (Hart-Celler Act). Replaces national origins quota system with visa programs that prioritize family reunification and U.S. labor needs.
1986	Immigration Reform and Control Act (IRCA). Makes employment of undocumented workers illegal, doubles the size of the U.S. Border Patrol, and enacts two legalization programs through which nearly three million undocumented people became lawful permanent residents.
1990	The 1990 Immigration Act. Expands employment-based visas and terminates judges' discretion in deportation cases for criminal offenders.
1996	Illegal Immigration Reform and Immigrant Responsibility Act (IIRAIRA). Expands grounds for inadmissibility and deportation; increases the U.S. Border Patrol, reduces public benefits available to lawful immigrants, and restricts eligibility for many immigration benefits.
1997	Nicaraguan Adjustment and Central American Relief Act (NACARA). The result of a lawsuit, it provides some benefits for select nationals of Nicaragua, Cuba, El Salvador, Guatemala, and former Soviet-bloc countries.
2001	The USA Patriot Act. Broadens grounds of inadmissibility based on suspected ties to terrorism; increases surveillance of foreign students.
2002	The Homeland Security Act. Creates the U.S. Department of Homeland Security and its three divisions—U.S. Citizenship and Immigration Services (USCIS), Customs and Border Protection (CPB), and Immigration and Customs Enforcement (ICE)—that now oversee the immigration system.
2005	The REAL ID Act. Expands grounds for inadmissibility and deportation; requires states to verify lawful status before issuing a driver license or State ID.
2006	The Secure Fence Act. Mandates the construction of 700 additional miles of fencing along the U.S.–Mexico border; allocates additional resources for border militariztion.
2012	Deferred Action for Childhood Arrivals (DACA). Executive Action that provides some protection from deportation to select undocumented youth between the ages of 15 and 30 who arrived in the U.S. before their 16th birthday; it also provides a work permit. Deportation protection and work eligibility are good for a two-year period and are renewable.
2014	Deferred Action for Parental Accountability (DAPA) and Expanded DACA. Currently under court injunction, DAPA would provide some protection from deportation for select parents of U.S. citizen and lawfully resident children for a period of three years; it also would provide a 3-year work permit. Expanded DACA would remove the upper age cap and extend the protection period and work eligibility to three years.

FIGURE 2.1 **Timeline of immigration policy.**
Adapted from the Migration Policy Institute Timeline of Major U.S. Immigration Laws, 1/90–Present.

Anya agreed to meet with me to discuss their possible participation in my research project. When Anya opened the door to their two-bedroom Evanston, Illinois, apartment, she greeted me with a hug. I liked her immediately, drawn, like Enrique, to her strong and open personality.

We sat at their kitchen table, nibbling dark Russian chocolate and sipping coffee as we talked. Enrique was not there—he was still in Mexico, waiting for a decision on their case. Anya missed him. She was resentful that they were being kept apart and angry that she was powerless to bring him home; Anya is not a woman accustomed to feeling powerless. I asked her about herself, her background, and her relationship with Enrique. Anya began telling me her story, a story that would unfold over the course of several days and span continents and decades, weaving together complex global histories and national politics into a personal tale of her and Enrique's struggle to be a family.

Neither Enrique nor Anya was born in the United States. They both left their homelands in the 1990s with next to nothing, fleeing disadvantage and a crumbling social structure. They both migrated with members of their family, Anya with her parents and Enrique with his first wife, to join friends who promised them a safer, more prosperous future in the United States. Both spent many a night during their journey unsure where the next day would take them, and they both arrived in the United States with little money, no English language skills, and few social connections.

The similarities in their stories end there. Anya left her home in the former Soviet Union to escape anti-Semitism; she was processed in Europe as a U.S. refugee and arrived in the United States legally, by plane. Enrique left his home in Mexico to escape poverty; he was ineligible for refugee status and unable to get a visa to come to the United States. He arrived in the United States illegally by walking across the U.S.–Mexico border. With refugee status, Anya's family was eligible for government assistance, including housing and job placement services. With no status, Enrique was ineligible to work lawfully and barred from receiving all social services except emergency medical care. Five years after their arrival, Anya and her parents became naturalized U.S. citizens. Enrique remained undocumented for nearly 15 years and, as you will see, changing his status cost him and Anya dearly.

At first glance, the differences in Anya and Enrique's statuses seem straightforward: some people are U.S. citizens; others are legal immigrants such as refugees or permanent residents; and still others have no status and are undocumented. Yet this apparent simplicity masks a more complex reality: U.S. immigration laws are ever changing, embedded in broader sociopolitical contexts, and can leave whole populations of people with either an ambiguous status or no status at all. This raises several questions of anthropological interest: Why do some families qualify for legal status whereas others do not? Who gets to decide, and how are their decisions connected to wider political, economic, and social concerns? More generally, why is it that people from some nations can travel the world with relative ease, whereas borders and laws confine others to their homelands?

Insofar as immigration policies regulate who is welcome in a nation-state and who is not, they reflect dominant ideas about what the nation is and what it ought to be. As these ideas shift, so too do immigration and citizenship policies, including and excluding different groups over time. In the United States, immigration and citizenship have historically been tied to concerns about the racial, class, and gendered composition of the nation-state. For Anya and Enrique and millions of others, immigration policies and the values that underpin them tend to favor some immigrants and not others, differently shaping migrants' abilities to enter and stay in the United States legally. Thus, to fully understand the current process of legalization, we must also understand the historical process of illegalization: who gets in, who is kept out, and why?

This chapter reviews the historical development of the U.S. immigration system. I begin with the first U.S. citizenship policy—established a mere 7 years after the United States became a nation-state—and track major changes to immigration and citizenship policies over the following 220 years, ending in the second decade of the 21st century with a discussion of immigration programs in the current period. This is a long and complex history, and I have narrowed the focus to how major shifts in U.S. immigration and citizenship policies have been shaped by dominant ideas about race, class, and gender and sexuality. And although I try to show how these threads interconnect the experiences of different U.S. immigrants, as well as the experiences of citizens and noncitizens, I emphasize the ways in which U.S. immigration policies have affected Mexicans, since this history lays necessary groundwork for later chapters.

The History of the Politics and the Politics in the History

At their core, immigration and citizenship policies codify sociopolitical concerns with ancient origins: who are "we," who are "they," and who decides? The formation of modern nation-states at the end of the colonial period gave these questions a distinctly national character: who are we, *as a nation*? Immigration and citizenship policies are often conceptualized as "nation-building" projects in that they legitimize the control of states over national territories and consolidate national membership with a shared political identity, such as "American" or "U.S. citizen." Nation-building is apparent both in the assumptions that underlie immigration policies—such as the idea that state governments have a right, or even a mandate, to establish national boundaries and control the movement of people over them—and in their concrete manifestations, such as the requirement that immigrants learn English and mainstream U.S. civic history before they can naturalize as U.S. citizens.

Although immigration and citizenship policies both regulate who "belongs," politically speaking, in a nation-state, they do it in distinct ways. Typically, immigration policies determine who can legally enter and remain in a national territory, whereas citizenship policies confer certain rights on some of those people and not on others. That is, there can be and often is a mismatch between the people who are legally present in a nation-state and those who are allowed to be its citizens. In the current period, this mismatch is additionally layered by multiple categories of noncitizens, including legal residents, temporary migrants, the undocumented, and those with some kind of "in-between" status, like DACA or temporary protected status (Menjívar 2006). This complex configuration gives rise to a social hierarchy in which law excludes specific groups from the attainment and/or exercise of citizenship, denying them certain rights and leaving them politically disempowered and vulnerable to insecurity, exploitation, and deportation.

Free White Men of Good Moral Character: Policy of the 18th and 19th Centuries

To understand the U.S. immigration system as it works today, it is helpful to go back to its roots. When the United States emerged as a sovereign nation-state in the late 18th century, ideas about citizenship took shape amid concerns about asserting independence from Great Britain and legitimizing the rule of new, national elites. The young nation-state expanded its territory rapidly through a series of aggressive military campaigns and dubious treaties, pushing westward to the Mississippi River by 1802 and, with the military conquest of Mexico's northern territories, arriving at the Pacific Ocean by the mid-19th century. The conquest of Mexicans in the West, enslavement of African Americans in the South, and the displacement of Native Americans throughout the territories was driven by rhetoric of "American exceptionalism" and beliefs about the racial superiority of white Christian citizenry. The earliest U.S. citizenship policies were designed in this context to uphold U.S. claims to Native American lands and to legitimize subjugation of slaves, women, Mexicans, and poor whites.

The first major citizenship policy in the United States was the Naturalization Act of 1790. The 1790 act restricted naturalization as a U.S. citizen to "free white men of good moral character," upholding not only prevailing racial and gendered ideas about citizenship, but also class-based criteria. The condition of "free white men" restricted citizenship to white male landholders who were economically independent; in contrast, slaves, women, and poor whites were considered "dependent" and incapable of self-sufficiency and, thus, self-governance (Nakano Glenn 2002). The criterion of "good moral character" was key to the exclusion of poor white men from citizenship, since good moral character was (and is) largely defined in opposition to activities associated with poor people, such as loitering, theft, vice, and gambling. These prohibitions were central to the creation of what Thomas Jefferson called a "responsible and virtuous electorate" (in Nakano Glenn 2002, 27), characterized by the amalgamation of whiteness, wealth, and political empowerment.

Legal barriers to citizenship for working-poor white men were lifted by the mid-19th century, when property ownership ceased to be a prerequisite to voting (Nakano Glenn 2002). As class-based barriers to U.S. citizenship diminished over the course of the 19th century and women gained the right to vote by 1920, racial dimensions of immigration and citizenship policy became more specific and important.

When it ended in 1848, the Mexican–American war had been the deadliest and costliest war in U.S. history (Gutierrez 1995). According to the stipulations of the Treaty of Guadalupe Hidalgo, Mexico ceded its entire northern province to the United States, along with the 75,000 to 100,000 Mexicans who resided there (De Genova and Ramos-Zayas 2003; Gutierrez 1995, 13). Treaty stipulations also guaranteed that

Mexicans living in the conquered territory would have access to U.S. citizenship. This was accomplished not by expanding U.S. citizenship to include nonwhites, but by legally classifying Mexicans as white (Gutierrez 1995).

Despite their legal "whiteness," Mexicans were widely regarded with derision and steadily relegated them to an inferior "castelike" status in the developing social structure of the U.S. Southwest (Cardoso 1980; De Genova and Ramos-Zayas 2003; Gutierrez 1995; Pedraza and Rumbaut 1996). Mexican Americans were steadily displaced from their lands, subject to civil rights violations, and forced into low-wage, low-status work in agriculture, mining, and construction (De Genova 2005; Gutierrez 1995). In a system sometimes called "Juan Crow" segregation, Mexicans were also racially segregated from whites in housing, schooling, and public facilities throughout the Southwest (Gutierrez 1995; Menchaca and Valencia 1990); this segregation was justified by a doctrine of white racial supremacy that cast Mexicans as simple-minded racial "hybrids" (Cardoso 1980; Menchaca and Valencia 1990; Pedraza and Rumbaut 1996). By the turn of the century, occupational discrimination became institutionalized into a dual-wage system, in which Mexican workers were consistently paid less than their white counterparts (Gutierrez 1995; Hondagneu-Sotelo 1994). And although the legal "whitening" of Mexicans exempted them from the wholesale denial of citizenship that applied to "nonwhites" at the time, their designation as U.S. citizens would be both legally contested and politically undermined for much of the next century and a half.

Following the abolition of slavery in 1865, there was intense debate in the U.S. Congress surrounding what rights should be granted to free blacks. An 1857 Supreme Court decision denied citizenship to African Americans, and the Chief Justice, Roger B. Taney, decreed that "Negroes had no rights that white people were bound to respect" (Ngai 2004). The Civil Rights Act of 1866 and the 14th Amendment to the U.S. Constitution (1868) overruled that decision. These acts extended citizenship to most people born in the United States (except for Native Americans), including people of African descent. Yet the promise of U.S. citizenship rang hollow for many African Americans. In fact, although many free blacks had been able to vote at the beginning of the century, their citizenship rights eroded during the following decades, and many African Americans were prevented from exercising citizenship rights for much of the next century. Meanwhile, the "black codes" and newly passed vagrancy laws were used as a pretext to return free blacks across the South to plantation work as inmates (Blackmon 2009; Nakano Glenn 2002; Perkinson 2010), foreshadowing patterns of today's mass incarceration and detention systems (Alexander 2010; Gomberg-Muñoz 2012).

Despite early anti-immigrant sentiment directed mostly at Irish, Germans, and Scandinavians, the United States did not have an immigration system per se for most of the 19th century. The demand for immigrant labor was great, and working-poor Europeans came to the United States by the millions to feed the industrial boom in growing cities of the North and Midwest. There was no numerical restriction on immigration, but new arrivals were personally inspected at Ellis and Angel Islands and could be denied entry for things like mental and physical "deficiency" (Gould 1981). Still, rates of exclusion of arriving European immigrations were low—only about 1 percent of the 25 million new immigrants who arrived between 1880 and World War I were turned away (Ngai 2004, 18).

In the rush to settle the U.S. Southwest following the Mexican–American War, Chinese workers were imported as agricultural labor and used to build the railroads that would connect East with West. When the United States experienced an economic downturn in the 1870s, these workers were targeted with vigilante violence and growing anti-Chinese sentiment (Chacon and Davis 2006). The first restrictive immigration policy in the United States, the 1882 Chinese Exclusion Act, was directed at them. The Chinese Exclusion Act both barred the immigration of Chinese laborers and made them "racially ineligible" for U.S. citizenship. The persecution of Chinese workers spread to include Japanese landowners and Filipino farmworkers, and it had strongly gendered dimensions. Whereas Filipinos were vilified for their supposed sexually aggressive pursuit of white women, Asian women were widely associated with prostitution. In 1875, the Page Law prohibited the entry of Asian "prostitutes," and its effect was to hinder the entrance of nonelite Asian women more broadly (Gerken 2013).

In 1882, Congress also devised the first general immigration law, composed primarily of a head tax and the prohibition of people deemed "likely to become a public charge"—that is, to use welfare or other public services (Daniels 2001). This provision was effective at keeping out the poor and infirm, as well as single women and disabled people (Cacho 2012), and it has remained a key part of the U.S. immigration statute (Immigration and Nationality Act [INA] § 212). By the 1910s, grounds for exclusion had expanded to include convicts, "idiots," and "lunatics," as well as anyone who failed a literacy test or had someone else pay for their passage to the United States (Gerken 2013). All of these provisions disproportionately excluded working-poor immigrants.

In 1917, the Asiatic Barred Zone Act was passed. It extended the bar on Chinese immigration and citizenship to all Southern and Eastern Asians except for the Japanese (who were prevented from immigrating by a "Gentleman's Agreement" signed in 1908) and Filipinos, since the Philippines was then a U.S. colony (Ngai 2004). As in earlier periods, these restrictions contained racial, class, and gendered components. Asians who were ineligible for citizenship were also barred from owning property in many states, and U.S.-citizen women who married one of these "ineligible" immigrants could have their U.S. citizenship revoked (Nakano Glenn 2002). The 1917 act also added "homosexuals," as well as alcoholics, anarchists, and polygamists, to the growing list of excludable immigrants.

As prohibitions on Asian immigration led to agricultural labor shortages, U.S. businesses increasingly turned to Mexican workers for their labor needs (Massey 2009). To tap this labor reserve, recruiters traveled deep into the heart of Mexico's populated north-central valleys, where they enlisted Mexicans to work in agriculture, construction, and industry across the U.S. Southwest and in cities such as Chicago, Cleveland, and Pittsburgh (De Genova and Ramos-Zayas 2003). By the 1920s, Mexican workers (both migrants and Mexican Americans) comprised as much as 75 percent of the agricultural workforce in California and the unskilled construction labor force in Texas (Gutierrez 1995, 34). By this time, Chicago's Mexican community had grown into the largest population of Mexicans outside of the U.S. Southwest (Ready and Brown-Gort 2005), and Mexican workers constituted 43 percent of all railroad track labor and 11 percent of employees in steel and meatpacking plants in the Chicago area (De Genova 2005, 114).

With this growing reliance on low-paid Mexican workers, Mexicans in the United States became widely associated with manual labor. Stereotypes of Mexicans as "dirty" and unambitious, but usually industrious, workers spread (Nakano Glenn 2002). Mexicans were considered especially desirable as workers because of their propensity to return to Mexico (Gutierrez 1995), and the proximity of Mexico to the United States made it relatively easy to deport Mexican workers when their labor was no longer in high demand.

The recruitment of Mexican and Filipino immigrant workers was also a highly gendered practice. In fact, as Filipino and Mexican men were enticed to come work in the United States, their female counterparts were often subject to restriction and deportation. The strategy of keeping out women was intended to discourage permanent settlement and biological reproduction of communities that were desired for their labor but not for national membership (Golash-Boza and Hondagneu-Sotelo 2013). But the exclusion of women also fed into fears that immigrant men of color were sexual deviants bent on pursuing white women—fears that drove violent attacks against Filipino farm workers in the 1920s (Chacon and Davis 2006).

The Quota System and the Bracero Program: 1924 to 1964

At the turn of the 20th century, European immigration to the United States was still largely unrestricted, and millions of working-poor immigrants from Southern and Eastern Europe arrived in the United States between 1890 and 1920. This immigration stream caused great anxiety among U.S. policy makers, and it led to the first general immigration policy in the United States.

Congressional debates about immigration at this time were guided by the ideology of eugenics, which erroneously attributed human social and behavioral differences to genetic traits and grouped people into distinct "races" that could be hierarchically ordered from superior to inferior (Gould 1981). Eugenicists found that new immigrants from Italy, Poland, Hungary, and Russia were "defective stock" and inalterably inferior to the "Nordic races" of Northern and Western Europe (Gould 1981). Worse, their innate "feeble-mindedness" led to high rates of criminality and weak morality, culminating in dangerously high fertility levels likely to be mixed with "Negro" blood (Chavez 2008; Gould 1981). The congressman Albert Johnson, chair of the House Immigration Committee and head of the Eugenics Research Association, warned his congressional colleagues that "inassimilable . . . filthy, un-American, and often dangerous" Jews would overrun the United States if their immigration remained unchecked (in Daniels 2001, 20).

Johnson's solution to this immigration "problem" was a bill that he chiefly authored, the Johnson–Reed Act of 1924. The 1924 act was a landmark immigration bill that placed widespread restrictions on U.S. immigration for the first time. The act restricted annual visa allotments to 2 percent of the "national origins" of the U.S. population of

1890, based on that year's census data (Ngai 2004). The national-origins quota system was designed to create immigration patterns that more closely reproduced the desired racial composition of the United States, and the census data were manipulated accordingly. The 1890 census, rather than that of 1920, was selected because it was before the height of immigration from Southern and Eastern Europe. Further, all non-white populations in the United States—including "immigrants from the New World and their descendants [i.e. Latin Americans]; any Asians or their descendants; the descendants of 'slave immigrants' [i.e. African Americans]; and the descendants of 'American aborigines' [i.e. Native Americans]"—were excluded from the quota system altogether (Daniels 2001, 22).

The end result of the 1924 act was that 84 percent of all U.S. visas were granted to Northern and Western Europeans, and racial bars on immigration and citizenship of Asians were left intact (Ngai 2004). Johnson celebrated the act's passage by proclaiming that "the United States is our land. . . . We intend to maintain it so. The day of indiscriminate acceptance of all races has definitely ended" (in Daniels 2001, 23). The U.S. president Calvin Coolidge declared that "America must be kept American" as he signed the act into law and further cemented into place the conflation of race and nation in U.S. immigration policy (in Gould 1981).

Notably, Latin Americans were exempted from numerical restriction under the 1924 act to satisfy demands for their labor in the U.S. Southwest (Gutierrez 1995; Ngai 2004). Neither guaranteed visas by the quota system nor excluded from immigration altogether, Mexican migrants could be recruited in times of high labor demand, such as the harvest season, and then restricted and "repatriated" in the off-season. To rationalize this practice, Mexicans were characterized as a labor force whose racial characteristics made them ideally suited to arduous and low-paying agricultural work (Gutierrez 1995; Pedraza and Rumbaut 1996). By 1930, the U.S. Census Bureau officially established "Mexican" as a distinct racial category (De Genova 2005, 221), and throughout the 1930s, criminalization and deportation of Mexicans was explicitly based on race and not citizenship (De Genova and Ramos-Zayas 2003, 5; Pedraza and Rumbaut 1996). During the Great Depression, for example, some 500,000 people of Mexican descent were deported from the United States, as many as half of whom were native-born U.S. citizens (Balderrama and Rodriguez 2006; Daniels

2001). The 1924 act did require Mexicans to pay a head tax and avoid being deemed likely to become a public charge, but in all, restrictions on Asian and Southern and Eastern European immigration would make Mexican labor more important to the U.S. economy in the decades to come (Daniels 2001).

The significance of Mexican labor in the U.S. economy was fomented by the onset of World War II. As women and southern African Americans were recruited to work in industry throughout the north, Mexican workers were imported en masse to the U.S. Southwest, where they harvested the food that would sustain industrial workers and the families of soldiers abroad. To ensure an unhindered labor supply, the United States and Mexico signed a binational treaty in 1942 that came to be known as the Bracero Program. The Bracero Program was a contract worker program that brought an estimated 5 million workers from Mexico to labor in the agricultural fields, construction sites, and factories across the southwestern United States and in cities such as Chicago (De Genova and Ramos-Zayas 2003). The program was initially conceived as an emergency wartime measure, but it proved to be so important that Congress extended it several times before it was finally terminated in 1964—after a period of 22 years.

Many migrant workers came in and out of the Bracero Program, sometimes migrating as braceros and other times migrating as undocumented workers (De Genova and Ramos-Zayas 2003). In 1954, the U.S. government launched "Operation Wetback," a high-profile campaign designed to curb undocumented migration and funnel more migrant workers through the Bracero Program. In a tag-team effort, U.S. immigration agents transported undocumented workers to the U.S.–Mexico border, where U.S. Department of Labor officials were waiting to process some of the deportees and send them back to the United States as braceros (Massey et al. 2002). Ultimately, the duration and scale of the Bracero Program dramatically increased the interconnections between the U.S. economy and Mexican workers, establishing a migration pattern that could endure with or without the benefit of access to visas (Massey et al. 2002).

The Immigration and Nationality Act of 1965

By midcentury, the explicitly racist nature of U.S. immigration policy was being eroded by several factors, including the fight against fascism in Nazi Germany (which led to a political distancing from eugenics), the civil rights movement, and a general turn toward more progressive social thinking on race and racism. In 1946, Congress eased some of the restrictions on Asian immigration, and in 1952, the McCarran–Walter Act finally lifted racial bars to U.S. citizenship for Asian immigrants and Native Americans and prioritized family reunification in immigration law (Daniels 2001). Notably, the 1952 act also specified that "homosexuals" could be excluded on the grounds of mental defectiveness—a response to antigay sentiment in the United States at the time (Gerken 2013).

In the 1960s, the Civil Rights Act (1964) and the Voting Rights Act (1965) significantly expanded the ability of African Americans to exercise their citizenship rights. Then, in 1965, at the height of the civil rights movement, the INA was passed. The 1965 INA replaced the existing national-origins quota system with per country caps on immigration and a preference system for family reunification and U.S. labor needs. The INA's passage was celebrated as the dawn of a new era in U.S. immigration policy—one that moved away from the explicitly race-based immigration policies of the past. Although the INA was immigration legislation, it was widely considered an extension of civil rights legislation (Lee 1999).

However, as Congress debated the 1965 bill, it became clear to many observers that the elimination of the national origins quota system was not meant to wholly transform existing immigration patterns. Lawmakers who spoke in support of the bill touted redressing historic wrongs done to Southern and Eastern Europeans, but not to Asians or Latinos, and immigration experts assured policy makers that the new system would not substantially increase immigration from Asia or otherwise alter established immigration patterns, suggesting that racial concerns about immigration remained alive, if unspoken (Daniels 2001; Lee 1999). In addition, the 1965 INA also explicitly barred gays and lesbians (and other so-called "sexual perverts") from immigrating to the United States (Gerken 2013).

Despite reassurances to Congress, passage of the 1965 bill did transform U.S. immigration patterns. Asian immigration quadrupled between 1960 and 1980, as Asians took advantage of their newfound ability to get U.S. visas primarily through employment programs (Nakano Glenn 2002; Ngai 2004). African immigration also increased, but it remained a small proportion of the total (Daniels 2001). Although it is often claimed that Mexican immigration dramatically increased following 1965 (e.g. Daniels 2001), calculations of Mexican immigration rarely include the cyclical but long-standing migration of millions of braceros between 1942 and 1964. Including bracero workers substantially levels the rate of Mexican immigration over time and changes the "dramatic" increase to a more modest one (Massey et al. 2002). However, the migration patterns of Mexicans and Filipinos did shift from largely cyclical labor migration toward more year-round, permanent family settlement (Chavez 1988).

Despite the economic and social ties that proliferated during the Bracero Program, the 1965 INA did not expand the availability of visas for Latin Americans, but reduced it (De Genova 2004). This is because the INA put caps on migration from Mexico and other Latin American nations for the first time ever—just one year after the Bracero Program ended. Between 1965 and 1980, the number of visas available to Latin Americans was reduced from an unlimited number to just 20,000 per country per year (Nakano Glenn 2002). These restrictions did not ultimately curb the migration of Latin Americans to the United States, but they did make it far more difficult for them to migrate legally (Massey 2009). In effect, barriers to legal status in the context of long-standing and ever-increasing migration patterns fomented undocumented migration in the decades that followed.

Indeed, although the 1965 INA was largely considered a civil rights win, the new system was poorly suited to address uneven demands for U.S. visas rooted in colonial histories and accelerating global ties. China got the same number of visas as Bali, and Mexico got the same number as Belgium. The result is that countries with stronger connections to the United States (not to mention bigger populations) saw their demand for U.S. visas quickly exceed the supply. Lines for U.S. visas began to form and then lengthen, especially in Mexico, China, India, and the Philippines. The result is that even people with U.S.-citizen relatives have little chance of quickly attaining a U.S. immigrant visa from one of these "oversubscribed" nations. It is no coincidence that nationals from these places comprise most of the undocumented population in the United States today.

A Nation of Borders: The 1980s and 1990s

After the 1965 act, explicit mention of race has all but disappeared from immigration policy debates. In its place, "illegal immigration" has become the chief political target of U.S. immigration policy. As with previous periods, restrictions on immigration are conceptually and administratively tied to concerns about criminality, lack of assimilation, and "retaining" America's heritage, but now these map onto an immigration classification, "illegal alien," that is legally—but not socially or politically—divorced from ethnoracial associations.

Amid growing concerns about "illegal immigration" and an "out of control [southern] border," congressional plans to restrict immigration arose once again in the 1980s. As Congress debated new legislation to curb unlawful immigration from Mexico, Senator Alan Simpson claimed, "These new persons *and their descendants* do not assimilate satisfactorily. . . . They may well create in America the same social, political, and economic problems that exist in the countries from which they have chosen to depart" (in Daniels 2001, 51; emphasis added). Although Simpson did not invoke race explicitly, this statement is reminiscent of Johnson's 1924 description of inassimilable and dangerous Jews, and its suggestion that assimilation is heritable by children suggests that racial concerns about this new, and mostly nonwhite, immigrant "influx" persisted.

In 1986, Simpson cosponsored the first immigration bill that targeted undocumented people: the Immigration Reform and Control Act, or IRCA. IRCA made the employment of undocumented workers illegal for the first time, although provisions in the law largely protected employers from prosecution (Calavita 1994; Massey et al. 2002). IRCA also doubled funding for the Border Patrol, but it included an amnesty provision through which some 2.7 million undocumented people were able to legalize their status (Calavita 1994; Meyers 2005; Rytina 2002). In 1987, a "Family Fairness" executive action extended protection from deportation to children whose parents were legalizing under IRCA and was broadened to include spouses of IRCA applicants in 1990 (American Immigration Council 2014). Then, in 1990, the 1965 INA was modified to increase total immigration and create new temporary visa categories for high-skill workers (Leiden and Neal 1990).

A decade later, concerns about immigrant criminality and the dangers posed by "multiculturalism," the ideological flip side of assimilation, gained congressional attention once again (Gerken 2013). In 1996, Congress passed the Illegal Immigration Reform and Immigrant Responsibility Act (IIRAIRA), which is widely considered the most punitive and draconian U.S. immigration bill to date. The IIRAIRA put measures in place that blocked many undocumented people from ever changing their immigration status, and it facilitated the deportation of lawful permanent residents. I discuss IIRAIRA's effects on legalization in more depth later, but since IIRAIRA, the rate of deportation of non-citizens has increased nearly eightfold, from 50,924 in 1995 to 393,289 in 2009 (U.S. Department of Homeland Security 2013). About 10 percent of deportees are lawful permanent residents who, as a result of IIRAIRA, could be deported for even minor offenses (Baum et al. 2010). IIRAIRA was also applied retroactively, so that lawful permanent residents who committed crimes as teenagers could be deported decades later, regardless of their family ties or subsequent behavior (Coutin 2007). Finally, IIRAIRA required that U.S. citizens and lawful residents who petition for a relative earn 125 percent or more of the federal poverty level and agree to take financial responsibility for their arriving family member for at least five years, reflecting continued concerns about the class characteristics of new immigrants (Gerken 2013).

The 1990s also marked a major shift toward militarization of the U.S.–Mexico border. Throughout the 1990s, the U.S. Border Patrol built miles of steel fencing, new roads, and lighting along the border that was guarded with hundreds of new agents and high-tech detection systems (Meyers 2005). The Border Patrol also launched a series of highly publicized "operations" on the U.S.–Mexico border, which made unauthorized border crossings more dangerous (Chacon and Davis 2006; Massey et al. 2002). Like caps on visas, border militarization has not stopped migration, but it has rerouted migrant trails from more populated areas into vast stretches of desert, pushing the cost and risk of unauthorized border crossing to the ceiling (De León 2015; Jimenez 2009).

The timing of IIRAIRA and U.S. border militarization is especially relevant because the 1990s also ushered in a proliferation of free trade agreements between the United States and Mexico that added millions of Mexicans to the rolls of mobile wage seekers (Delgado Wise and Cypher 2007). These agreements, such as the General Agreement on Tariffs and Trade (entered into by Mexico in 1986) and the North American Free Trade Agreement (NAFTA; 1994), lifted restrictions on the movement of capital, goods, money, and businesses at the same time that IIRAIRA and border operations restricted the movement of Mexican workers (Massey et al. 2002). Free trade agreements devastated the working and living conditions of many Mexicans, as cheap, mass-produced U.S. grains and goods flooded Mexican markets, pushing farmers off their land and undermining the ability of Mexican craftspeople to sell their wares. The Mexican economy contracted in the 1980s and again, following NAFTA's passage, in the 1990s; the Mexican peso fell to a fraction of its pre-1970 value, whereas unemployment, debt, and crime all rose precipitously (Greider 1997). After 100 years of migration, Mexican workers faced historic restrictions on their movement at the same time that free trade agreements undermined their ability to stay home and make a living as workers, farmers, and small business owners. Mexican migration continued, but with legal avenues restricted, it became ever more characterized as illegal.

Immigration policy changes in the 1990s had complex sexual, racial, and gendered dimensions. The outright prohibition on gay and lesbian immigrants was finally lifted in 1990 (Gerken 2013), although the family visa system was not adapted to allow U.S. citizens and lawful residents to petition for their same-sex partners until 2013. Meanwhile, the concentration of immigration enforcement on the U.S.–Mexico border strengthened the association of "illegal immigration" with Latin Americans and with Mexicans in particular (De Genova 2005), although about half of the undocumented population enters the United States legally with a temporary visa.

Anti-immigrant policies of the 1990s often especially targeted Latina women (Chavez 2008; Golash-Boza and Hondagneu-Sotelo 2013). Reminiscent of the rhetoric surrounding the "yellow peril" of the 19th century and the "European scourge" of the early 20th, Latinas in the 1990s were disparaged as "breeders" of "anchor babies" who drained public resources away from more "deserving" (and presumably more sexually reserved) U.S. citizens (Chavez 2008). Latina mothers were even suspected of instigating a population reconquest of the U.S. Southwest through their unrestrained baby-making (Huntington 2004; see Chavez 2008). In 1994, Californians voted to deny undocumented mothers access to prenatal care, as well as social services and education for their U.S.-born (and thus U.S.-citizen) children, although this measure was later declared unconstitutional. Two years later, and the same year as IIRAIRA, welfare reform measures cut access to public services for lawfully present immigrant women and reaffirmed an association of poverty with a lack of responsibility and racialized immorality (Chang 2000; Gerken 2013).

Expanded Enforcement: 2000 to 2015

As of 2015, no comprehensive immigration bill has passed at the federal level since IRCA, and in this legislative vacuum, U.S. immigration programs have prioritized enforcement. Following the attacks on the World Trade Center and the Pentagon on September 11, 2001, immigration enforcement came under the auspices of the DHS and its Immigration and Customs Enforcement division (ICE), signaling a broader shift toward the association of undocumented migration with terrorism and the criminalization of undocumented immigrants. Since then, immigration enforcement has expanded at both national and local levels, with interior enforcement roughly quadrupling in the five years from 2005 to 2010 (Heyman 2010).

In 2006, the DHS began to fund an enforcement program known as "Secure Communities." Secure Communities links the databases of local police agencies with the DHS and Federal Bureau of Investigation. When a person is arrested and fingerprinted, his or her fingerprints are run through the DHS database and, if there is a "hit" (often the result of being caught at the border), ICE can deport the individual regardless of whether he or she is ever charged or convicted of a crime. In fact, although ICE states that it targets "dangerous criminals," many deportations from the U.S. interior result from simple traffic stops (Zamudio 2011). This is a major change from long-standing enforcement practices, which were largely confined to the U.S.–Mexico border region. As a result of Secure Communities, any contact with police anywhere in the United States can, and increasingly does, end in deportation. In November 2014, Barack Obama announced that his administration would replace Secure Communities with a more "targeted" interior enforcement program; whether the new measure will ease the terror in immigrant communities across the United States remains to be seen.

In addition to federal programs like Secure Communities, states and municipalities have increasingly pursued their own immigration-related agendas. Nearly 1,600 pieces of immigration legislation were introduced at state capitols in the first eight months of 2011 alone—an all-time record (National Conference of State Legislatures 2011). Punitive immigration policies have been enacted in Arizona, Georgia, Alabama, and South Carolina, whereas more "immigrant-friendly" bills granting in-state college tuition or driver licenses to undocumented immigrants have been implemented in California, Connecticut, Illinois, and Colorado. Immigration policy making has also broken the confines of federal and state legislative bodies and proliferated at the local level. Between 2006 and March 2011, ordinances targeting undocumented immigrants had been passed and/or considered in more than 130 U.S. cities (Varsanyi 2011). These policies seek to regulate and persecute everyday behaviors associated with undocumented immigrants, and they range from English-only laws, to limits on the number of adults who can reside in a household, to bans on sitting in public spaces.

Even with the dramatic expansion of interior enforcement measures, the bulk of immigration-related criminal prosecutions and deportations remain concentrated in the U.S.–Mexico border region (Light et al. 2014). By 2012, criminal prosecutions for immigration violations made up more than half of all federal charges brought by the U.S. government; prosecutions for unlawful reentry accounted for nearly half of this growth (Light et al. 2014). And nearly three-quarters of prosecutions for unlawful reentry occurred in just five districts, all of which share a border with Mexico (Light et al. 2014; Linker 2013). Because these prosecutions are concentrated on the U.S.–Mexico border, they disproportionately ensnare Latin American entrants, and the share of Latinos among federally sentenced offenders rose from 23 percent in 1992 to 48 percent in 2012 (Light et al. 2014). Criminal prosecution for unlawful entry is but the latest iteration of the long-standing concentration of immigration enforcement measures on the U.S.–Mexico border, a practice that has helped to establish a broad association of Mexican immigrants with "illegality" and criminality in the United States (De Genova 2004; Massey 2009).

A final component of the immigration enforcement apparatus is the growing immigrant detention system. As of 2014, the United States had become home to an estimated 250 immigrant detention facilities—more than triple the number from 1996 (Detention Watch Network 2014). More than 30,000 immigrants, including children, are now held in detention on any given day. This number is driven by a congressional directive, called the "bed mandate," that sets a minimum quota of 34,000 immigrants that ICE must keep in detention per day (Miroff 2013).

The rapid and pervasive expansion of immigration enforcement in the first decades of the 21st century has had at least three major effects on undocumented people. First, it has helped push the U.S. deportation rate to record levels. For most of the 20th century, deportation rates fluctuated between 10,000 and 20,000 per year, reaching highs of 30,000 to 36,000 during the sweeps of the Great Depression (1924) and Operation Wetback (1954) (U.S. Department of Homeland Security 2013, 103). In 1997, one year after IIRAIRA, deportation rates reached more than 100,000 for the first time, and they have gone up steadily ever since. Between 1997 and 2012 alone, more than 4.2 million people were deported from the United States—more than double the total number of all prior deportations in the history of the United States (Golash-Boza and Hondagneu-Sotelo 2013).

Second, the threat of immigration enforcement has expanded from the U.S.–Mexico border, where it was long concentrated, to homes, worksites, and communities deep within the U.S. interior. The result is that many people picked up in the deportation dragnet have lived in the United States for many years, are members of mixed-status families, and have deep social connections in the United States.

Third, as states and localities implement their own brands of immigration-related policies, some friendly and others hostile, they have created a "patchwork quilt" landscape of policy and practice (Quesada et al. 2014) and intensified the significance of city, county, and state borders in the lives of undocumented people and their family members. Finally, a turn toward immigration enforcement has widely conflated unauthorized migration with immigrant criminality—an issue that I revisit in depth in Chapter 4.

Does Race Still Matter?

In the current period, immigration policies no longer openly target certain ethnoracial groups; rather, they target people who are unlawfully present. Because they are unlawfully present, the argument goes, undocumented people do not deserve the same rights and resources as lawful immigrants or U.S. citizens. Thus, immigration enforcement is largely considered consistent with the values of a "postracial" United States that offers "equal opportunity" for all. But are the policies that govern legal immigration and enforcement race neutral, or are they still guided by racial stereotyping? And is legal status a more legitimate basis for exclusion than race was, and how can we tell?

I consider the second question in the concluding chapter, but here I take a closer look at the first question: are immigration enforcement practices in a postracial United States still informed by ideas about race? Certainly, much of the rhetoric directed at undocumented people today sounds similar to racist stereotypes of earlier immigrant populations. Like their Irish, Chinese, Jewish, and Italian predecessors, today's unwanted immigrants are portrayed as an "invasion" of criminals, poor people, and baby makers who are incapable of assimilation and bent on degrading the United States to third-world status. Still, rhetoric aside, what evidence do we have that immigration practices are racist?

Although ICE has taken an official stance condemning racial profiling (U.S. Immigration and Customs Enforcement 2014b), emerging evidence indicates that U.S. immigration enforcement is permeated with racial, class, and gendered stereotyping (O'Leary and Sánchez 2011). For example, although deportations have increased for all national-origin groups since the 1990s, the rise has been especially sharp for Mexicans and Central Americans (Golash-Boza and Hondagneu-Sotelo 2013). Nationwide, immigrants from Latin America comprise about 75 percent of the total undocumented immigrant population, but they have accounted for more than 90 percent of deportees since 2000 (Fussell 2011; U.S. Department of Homeland Security 2013). Mexicans comprise 59 percent of the undocumented population, but have constituted between 65 and 80 percent of deportees each year between 2000 and 2009 (Fussell 2011; Passel and Cohn, 2009). Tanya Golash-Boza (2012b) found that Central American immigrants are many times more likely to be deported than Asians, who comprise just less than a quarter of the undocumented population; she reports that undocumented Hondurans have a 10 percent chance of being deported and undocumented Guatemalans have a 5 percent chance; in contrast, undocumented Vietnamese, Koreans, Filipinos, Indians, and Chinese all have less than a 1 percent chance of deportation (Golash-Boza 2012b, 89). And although deportation patterns reveal ethnoracial bias, their gender bias is especially pronounced: although roughly half of all undocumented people are women, more than 90 percent of deportees are men (Golash-Boza and Hondagneu-Sotelo 2013).

Because of the coupling of immigration and police agencies via Secure Communities and state-level policies, ethnoracial disparities in deportation rates are at least partially driven by local policing practices (Romero 2008). In 2011, for example, fully 93 percent of those detained through Secure Communities were Latino (Kohli et al. 2011). One study conducted in Irving, Texas, by the Chief Justice Earl Warren Institute found that, following the 2006 establishment of a partnership between local law enforcement and ICE, arrests of Latinos for minor offenses, particularly traffic violations, increased markedly. The study also found that local police arrested Latinos for misdemeanor offenses in significantly higher numbers than they arrested whites and African

Americans. The authors conclude that there is "strong evidence" to support the charge that local law enforcement officials used racial profiling of Latinos to screen them for immigration violations (Gardner and Kohli 2009).

In McHenry County, Illinois, a 2011 *Chicago Tribune* investigation found that county police officers were misreporting the race of people they stopped to hide widespread racial profiling and detention of Latinos. The *Tribune* analysis showed that in 2009, one in three Latinos was either mislabeled as white or omitted from department data altogether; if they were included, the department's official rate of minority stops would have been 65 percent higher than that in nearby Chicago (Mahr and McCoppin 2009). Because McHenry County is enrolled in ICE's Secure Communities program, anyone who is arrested by county police is automatically run through the DHS database; if there is a hit, that person may be detained and taken into custody by ICE, regardless of whether he or she is ultimately convicted of any crime. Thus, disproportionate arrests of Latinos in McHenry County increase their chance of deportation relative to other immigrant groups. Evidence for racial profiling of Latinos in areas where local police cooperate with immigration enforcement has also been found in Tennessee (Lacayo 2010) and North Carolina (Golash-Boza and Hondagneu-Sotelo 2013).

Together, the evidence suggests that immigration practice and race-based stereotypes are not so easily decoupled. This should not be surprising, since immigration agents and police officers do not work in bubbles, but are deeply integrated into the broader U.S. social fabric. In a society permeated with ethnoracial stereotypes and inequalities, the question is not "How could immigration practices still be racist?" The question is "How could they not be?"

Grounds for Inclusion

Even with extensive grounds for exclusion in place, the United States still grants some 1 million green cards to new immigrants each year (Zong and Batalova 2015). We have so far examined how dominant ideas about race, class, and gender have shaped grounds for exclusion—that is, how people are kept out. For the remainder of this chapter, I discuss contemporary criteria for inclusion: how people get in. Since the mid-20th century, almost everyone who lawfully immigrates to the United States attains his or her visa through one of four programs: family reunification, employment, humanitarian need, or a diversity lottery. And although these programs are ostensibly neutral, they still represent dominant ideas about who is, and who is not, welcome in the United States.

Family Reunification

Consistent with the post-1952 emphasis on family reunification, about two-thirds of all immigrant visas are issued to family members of U.S. citizens and lawful permanent residents. Visas for family members can be roughly divided into two groups. The first are for "immediate relatives" of adult U.S. citizens, which includes spouses, unmarried children under the age of 21, and parents. These immediate relatives are not subject to caps, so they can immigrate as soon as their paperwork is processed. (Remember, as I discuss in more depth later, undocumented people often cannot get these visas even with U.S.-citizen immediate relatives.) The second group of visas is allotted to other qualifying relatives, including adult children and siblings of U.S. citizens and spouses and minor children of lawful permanent residents. Visas for family members in this second group are subject to annual caps, with select family relationships ordered into a "preference system" that prioritizes some relationships over others. For these relatives, immigrating to the United States involves waiting "in line" for a visa to become available.

All countries get the same number of visas for preference relatives, and wait times for these visas range from a few months to more than two decades, depending on which "line" a person is in and how many of their co-countrymen are in that line already. For example, in July 2014, the U.S. Department of State was processing visa applications for adult unmarried children of U.S. citizens that had been filed in April 2007—an average worldwide wait time of 7 years. But for adult unmarried Filipino children of U.S. citizens, the Department of State was processing applications that had been filed in January 2003—an 11-year wait. Visa applications for adult unmarried Mexican children of U.S. citizens were being processed from February 1994—a whopping 20-year wait time for them. Paradoxically, the stronger the family ties between any particular country and the United States, the more demand there is for these visas and the longer people in those places will have to wait to be reunited with their U.S. family members. People from Mexico, India, China, and the Philippines face especially long lines, and it should not be surprising that

FAMILY-SPONSORED PREFERENCES

First: (**F1**) Unmarried Sons and Daughters of U.S. Citizens: 23,400 plus any numbers not required for fourth preference.

Second: Spouses and Children, and Unmarried Sons and Daughters of Permanent Residents: 114,200, plus the number (if any) by which the worldwide family preference level exceeds 226,000, plus any unused first preference numbers:

A. (**F2A**) Spouses and Children of Permanent Residents: 77% of the overall second preference limitation, of which 75% are exempt from the per-country limit;

B. (**F2B**) Unmarried Sons and Daughters (21 years of age or older) of Permanent Residents: 23% of the overall second preference limitation.

Third: (**F3**) Married Sons and Daughters of U.S. Citizens: 23,400, plus any numbers not required by first and second preferences.

Fourth: (**F4**) Brothers and Sisters of Adult U.S. Citizens: 65,000, plus any numbers not required by first three preferences.

On the chart below, the listing of a date for any class indicates that the class is oversubscribed (see paragraph 1); "C" means current, i.e., numbers are available for all qualified applicants; and "U" means unavailable, i.e., no numbers are available. (NOTE: Numbers are available only for applicants whose priority date is **earlier** than the cut-off date listed below.)

Family-Sponsored	All Chargeability Areas Except Those Listed	CHINA-mainland born	INDIA	MEXICO	PHILIPPINES
F1	01APR07	01APR07	01APR07	01FEB94	01JAN03
F2A	01MAY12	01MAY12	01MAY12	15MAR11	01MAY12
F2B	01MAY07	01MAY07	01MAY07	22NOV93	15AUG03
F3	15OCT03	15OCT03	15OCT03	00AUG93	22MAR93
F4	22DEC01	22DEC01	22DEC01	15DEC96	01JAN91

FIGURE 2.2 **Visa bulletin from July 2014.**

many people from these nations have forfeited the wait and attempted reunification with their U.S. family without the benefit of a visa.

Of course, this system also excludes anyone who does not have a qualifying U.S. relative. Take Enrique as an example. When Enrique migrated, he had several U.S.-citizen family members—an uncle, two cousins, and a nephew—but none of these relationships is connected to a U.S. visa program. Enrique also has a brother who lives in the United States, but because his brother is undocumented, Enrique's relationships with him and his U.S.-citizen sister-in-law and nephew do not count either. Finally, three years after his arrival in the United States, Enrique had a son, Julian, who is a U.S. citizen by birth. But Julian cannot file a visa petition for his father (or his mother) until he turns 21 years old. All told, despite his myriad connections to U.S. citizens, Enrique was ineligible for a family-based visa until he married Anya, and even then, his pathway to legal status was fraught with obstacles.

Employment

For hopeful immigrants who do not qualify for a family-based visa, a second option is employment-based immigration. Employment-based visas constitute about 16 percent of U.S. immigrant visas issued each year (Zong and Batalova 2015). Employment visas are primarily intended for people with "extraordinary abilities" in specified fields, or for athletes, entertainers, professors, multinational executives, and religious workers. The only category of employment visa that workers like Enrique qualify for is the "unskilled labor" category, for which 5,000 visas are allotted annually for the whole world.[1] Together, employment visas overwhelmingly favor highly educated, highly skilled, or otherwise extraordinary professionals and offer little opportunity for regular workers like Enrique.

This preference for professional classes is noteworthy given the long-standing dependence of the U.S. economy on low-paid immigrant labor—the very labor force that is mostly left out of the employment-based system. The demand for low-paid workers is not merely historical, but persists today, and in the absence of legal options for immigration is largely filled by temporary and undocumented workers. In fact, at 94 percent, undocumented men have higher labor force participation rates than U.S. citizens, and undocumented people comprise more than 10 percent of the U.S. workforce in industries such as agriculture (25 percent), groundskeeping and building maintenance (19 percent), construction (17 percent), and food preparation and service (12 percent) (Passel and Cohn 2009). As undocumented workers prop up the U.S. economy and subsidize the U.S. middle class with artificially low prices on food, child care, and other services, their immigration status keeps them from attaining higher education and better-paying employment (Chavez 2008; Gomberg-Muñoz 2011). That is, the current employment visa system does not seem to prevent the migration of low-paid workers so much as it keeps workers in low-paying positions by foreclosing their possibilities for legal immigration and any opportunities for upward mobility that legality affords.

Humanitarian Visas

For prospective immigrants who are ineligible for family-based or employment visas, another option is a humanitarian visa. Humanitarian visas account for about 12 percent of all U.S. visas (Zong and Batalova 2015) and they come in two forms: refugee and asylum. Refugees are processed outside of the United States and asylees are processed after they have already entered the United States. Humanitarian visas were developed during the Cold War period and are granted to applicants who can demonstrate a "well-founded fear of persecution" because of their race, membership in a social group, political opinion, religion, or national origin. But the determination of well-founded fear is not applied evenly, and the national origin of the applicant profoundly determines the outcome of a humanitarian visa application.

In fact, for Mexicans, the criterion of well-founded fear of persecution does not ever seem to apply. In 1998, the year that Enrique left Mexico, violence was on the rise because of a sudden and widespread degradation in living and working conditions following the passage of NAFTA. The murder rate was 14.1 per 100,000 people that year—nearly one and half times the rate that the United Nations considers "epidemic" (UN Office on Drugs and Crime 2013). Yet, the United States did not admit a single refugee from Mexico in 1998 (U.S. Department of Homeland Security 2013).

Following Mexico's economic crises of the 1980s and 1990s, violent crime spiked, driven by battles among and against Mexico's drug cartels. Mexico is the symbolic, if not actual, heart of drug trafficking in the Western Hemisphere—a result of its regrettable position between regional centers of drug manufacturing to the south and the global center of drug consumption, the United States, to the north. The former Mexican president Felipe Calderon has lamented, "We live next to the world's largest drug consumer, and all the world wants to sell them drugs through our door and our window. And we live next to the world's largest arms seller [the United States], which is supplying the criminals" (CNN World 2010). Calderon declared "war" on Mexico's drug cartels in 2006, and in the subsequent six years, Mexico was drowned in a massive, bloody internal war. More than 60,000 people were massacred and another 26,000 "disappeared" (Human Rights Watch 2013). At the height of this violence, in 2011, the homicide rate in Mexico spiked to 22.8 per 100,000 (UN Office on Drugs and Crime 2013), with Mexican government officials often acting in collaboration with narcogangs and implicated in the violence. And yet, the number of Mexican refugees admitted to the United States that year was zero (U.S. Department of Homeland Security 2013). In fact, from 2003 to 2012, the United States did not admit a single refugee from Mexico (ibid; see Boehm 2012).

In Honduras and El Salvador, extreme poverty, drug trafficking, and "gang" violence converge to produce some of deadliest cities in the Western Hemisphere. In 2011, Honduras's homicide rate dwarfed Mexico's, at 90 homicides per 100,000 people (UN Office on Drugs and Crime 2013). The number of Honduran refugees admitted to the United States in 2011 was 5 (U.S. Department of Homeland Security 2013). The number of Salvadorans admitted as refugees that year was zero (ibid). The number of Haitian refugees admitted to the United States after the 2010 earthquake that killed more than 200,000 people and displaced 1.5 million: just 18 (ibid). In fact, between 2003 and 2012, more than 99 percent of all refugee visas issued to Latin America and the Caribbean went to just two countries, Cuba and Colombia, with Cuba receiving the vast majority (ibid).

What makes Cuba so dangerous that it warrants a near monopoly on U.S. humanitarian visas in the Western Hemisphere? The answer is not immediately apparent. The homicide rate in Cuba is 4 per 100,000, one-fifth Mexico's rate and one-twentieth the rate of Honduras (UN Office on Drugs and Crime 2013). Cuba's homicide rate is even lower than that of the United States. According to the U.S. Department of State Bureau of Diplomatic Security, Cuba is safe for tourists, since "violent crime is not common" (U.S. Department of State 2015).

But as the immigration scholar Roger Daniels put it, "Immigration policy is a subset of foreign policy" (Daniels 2001, 35), and the decision to grant humanitarian visas overwhelmingly to Cubans while denying them to most other Latin Americans is deeply rooted in U.S. foreign policy concerns. Cuba, the home of a "socialist" government, represents the specter of communism in the Western Hemisphere. Since the 1950s, the United States has invaded Cuba militarily, placed it under embargo, and suspended diplomatic relations there. It has also welcomed with open arms hundreds of thousands of Cuban refugees fleeing communism. In fact, when unaccompanied Cuban children arrived in the United States after the Cuban Revolution in the 1960s, the U.S. government sanctioned a program known as *Pedro Pan* (Peter Pan) to welcome the children and help them get settled (Torres 2003). In contrast, when the U.S.-backed El Salvadoran government was involved in mass killing of civilians during its civil war in the 1980s, the United States overwhelmingly denied Salvadorans' applications for refugee status and asylum (Coutin 2007; Menjívar 2006). This blatantly discriminatory policy resulted in a successful lawsuit by Guatemalan and Salvadoran activists, which established some protections for Central Americans who had fled U.S.-funded violence in their homelands (Coutin 2000a, 2007). Yet this practice persists: in 2013 and 2014, tens of thousands of Central American children fleeing violence in their homelands arrived at the U.S.–Mexico border. Amid widespread calls to grant the children refugee status, Congress granted funds to expedite their deportation. Indeed, although U.S. military and economic intervention throughout Central America has helped catalyze mass emigration from the region, Central Americans have little chance of immigrating to the United States lawfully (Coutin 2000a, 2007; Golash-Boza 2012b).

The coupling of humanitarian visas to U.S. foreign policy agendas makes it far easier for some people to get these visas than others. Simply put, granting refugee status amounts to an acknowledgment that people are not protected by their government, and the United States is far more likely to acknowledge persecution by its political adversaries than by its allies (see Coutin 2007). Since Mexico is a close ally of the United States, Mexicans are unlikely to ever be granted humanitarian visas, regardless of the level of danger, persecution, or hardship that Mexicans face in their daily lives.

Diversity Immigrant Visa (the Green Card Lottery)

The last main option for legal immigration to the United States is the diversity visa lottery, which accounts for about 5 percent of all visas issued annually (Zong and Batalova 2015). Lottery visas are bonus visas allotted to people from regions with low rates of migration to the United States. To get a diversity visa, a person must first be a citizen of an "undersubscribed" nation. The overwhelming majority of diversity visas go to citizens of European and African countries; almost none go to North Americans (U.S. Department of State 2015). Applicants from qualifying nations are then randomly selected in a lottery drawing. A small number of diversity visas can go to people already residing in the United States provided they have an unexpired temporary visa. By definition, the diversity visa lottery is designed to expand diversity among U.S. immigrants, and it does not address or alleviate the backlog of demand for visas from Latin America and Asia.

In all, people like Enrique do not lack the knowledge or motivation to migrate legally—they lack the opportunity. The closure of pathways to legal immigration occurs in the context of a long-standing interrelationship between Mexican workers and U.S. society and economy that persists today. With possibilities to legal immigration foreclosed, Enrique joined millions of others who migrate without authorization and swell the ranks of the undocumented population in the United States.

Conclusion

Together, this review of the U.S. immigration system shows how immigration policies are neither rigid nor static, but built on the shifting sands of prevailing social values. As these values change over time, so too do the policies that are shaped by them. With the perspective of history, biases in law become apparent, and overt discriminatory policies that have targeted gays and lesbians, women, African Americans, Asians, and working-poor Europeans are no longer socially acceptable. Today, U.S. immigration policies sanction and enforce discrimination against undocumented people, a practice widely considered socially acceptable. Yet, the likelihood that a person will become and remain undocumented is tightly linked to U.S. economic and foreign policy strategies; moreover, emerging evidence suggests that immigration status and race are not easily unlinked: racial stereotypes continue to influence immigration in ideology and in practice.

This history also demonstrates that immigration and citizenship categories are not experienced uniformly. Instead, both U.S. citizenship and immigration statuses are nuanced with respect to the ethnoracial, gendered, and class characteristics of the status holder. Among U.S. citizens, the ability of racial minorities to exercise citizenship rights has been especially varied over time and periodically eroded or retracted. For lawful immigrants and the undocumented alike, vulnerability to immigration enforcement measures increases dramatically for Latino and Afro-Caribbean men (Golash-Boza and Hondagneu-Sotelo 2013). Thus, race, class, and gender discrimination form a common thread that connects the experiences of many U.S. groups, citizen and noncitizen alike.

Finally, despite meaningful shifts in U.S. immigration policy over time, this history also reveals some remarkable consistencies. Throughout U.S. history, welcome immigrants are imagined to more fully embody "American" values and traditions, whereas unwelcome immigrants are considered inassimilable and criminal—invaders who constitute a threat to both public safety and national identity. Immigrants' assimilation into American society is presumed to be not only desirable, but also innate and immutable and even inherited by offspring, rather than learned over time; the undertone of eugenics persists in these arguments. Legislatively, undesirable characteristics are glossed as a lack of "morality," attributing exclusion to personal characteristics of immigrants rather than to prevailing social values of the U.S. elite. Grounds for exclusion are accordingly adapted to exclude working-poor Asians of one generation and "sexual perverts" and "illegal Latinos" of the next. The division of potential immigrants into "desirable" and "undesirable" categories that are underpinned by racialized morality has a long history in the United States, and it is reinforced today in immigration processing. The remainder of this book explores how this reinforcement occurs.

CHAPTER 3

The Family Petition

Cynthia and Hector

Cynthia met Hector when she was a senior in high school. She was working part-time as a cashier at a small Chicago diner, where Hector's brother was the manager. Cynthia and Hector struck up a cautious friendship, speaking to each other at work functions or when Hector came into the diner to see his brother. After two years, they went on their first date.

Cynthia knew that Hector was undocumented, but she did not give it much thought at the time. Cynthia's parents were immigrants from Mexico themselves, and migration stories were an important and respected part of her family history. Cynthia's older sister had married an undocumented person in 2007, and they were able to legalize his status through consular processing. Cynthia assumed that she and Hector would do the same if they ever got married.

Although Cynthia was not especially concerned that Hector was undocumented, Hector was. He felt embarrassed by his status, and he worried that limits on his opportunities would also hold Cynthia back—a worry that became more pronounced as Cynthia graduated from college and then enrolled in medical school while Hector remained in a low-paid restaurant job. "Here you are, a medical student, and I'm working in the service sector," Hector would lament. "It was as if he felt less than me," Cynthia recalled. The shadow of his status affected their relationship in other ways as well. Cynthia wanted to drive when they went out, because she worried that Hector would get arrested for driving without a license. But driving was an important part of Hector's independence, and Cynthia tried to respect that, too. As the one "with papers," Cynthia began putting bills and property in her name as they consolidated their households. She felt the pressure of taking on the household responsibilities that Hector had to relinquish; the imbalance gnawed at both of them. Even in the absence of any dramatic encounters with police or immigration agents, the constraints associated with Hector's status marred their life together in subtle but ubiquitous ways.

After five years of dating, Cynthia and Hector got married in 2010. It was only then that the realization that Hector's constraints were hers, too, hit Cynthia hard. As the first person in her family to pursue an advanced degree, Cynthia saw no future for herself in Mexico. She worried that she might have to choose between her husband and her career if he got deported. She became anxious and depressed, trying to hide her feelings from Hector as she sought psychological counseling to manage her depression. And although she feared being separated from Hector, Cynthia agreed to begin the process to change Hector's immigration status.

Cynthia knew about consular processing as a result of her sister and brother-in-law's experience, and she knew that it was important to have a good attorney. As a first step, Cynthia made an appointment with the legal advisor at the university she attended. The advisor was "shocked" that Cynthia could not simply adjust her husband's status, and he could not recommend any attorneys who specialized in consular processing. Cynthia then turned to a friend of hers, a law school student, who recommended a highly respected immigration attorney who had written a book about immigration law. Cynthia and Hector booked a consultation with him. The attorney said that he was confident about their case; Hector had been arrested crossing the border but otherwise had a clean record, and the attorney assured them that USCIS had no reason to deny their petitions. Cynthia was still nervous and wanted to delay the process, but Hector was ready. Buoyed by the attorney's optimism, Cynthia and Hector began filing their paperwork for consular processing in the spring of 2011.

The first step involved filing a family petition, or I-130, which would make Hector eligible for a family-based visa. Cynthia and Hector gathered together dozens of documents: Hector's passport, both of their original birth certificates, Hector's parents' birth certificates, their original marriage certificate, photographs of their wedding, and documentation of joint bank accounts and shared household expenses. Their attorney mailed all of their documents and supporting materials to USCIS in April 2011. The attorney also filed an I-485, which is a petition to adjust Hector's status to lawful permanent U.S. resident. One month later, they received a notice from USCIS stating that their I-485 had been denied and that Hector had 30 days to leave the United States "voluntarily" or face deportation.

Shocked, they asked their attorney for an explanation. They eventually learned that Hector did not qualify to adjust his status with I-485 because he had entered the United States unlawfully; when the attorney tried to adjust Hector's status within the country instead of sending him to the U.S. consulate in Mexico, a removal order was triggered. The law had changed in 2001, 10 years prior, and the attorney was unaware of it. The good news, he informed them, was that they would still be able to pursue consular processing from Mexico. Hector and Cynthia called a family meeting and explained to Hector's parents and siblings—all of whom live in Chicago—that Hector had to leave abruptly for Mexico. Cynthia took a leave of absence from medical school so that she could go with him.

Cynthia and Hector spent the summer of 2011 in Mexico City trying to move forward with their immigration case. Their relationship was "very rocky" at this point, Cynthia says. She felt responsible for having chosen the attorney whose mistake banished Hector from his home and family in Chicago. She also felt distant from Hector, who had begun spending his days alone on his family's ranch to give her time to study. In August, Cynthia returned to Chicago, alone, to begin another semester of school. Abruptly, their attorney resigned their case to take a promotion at his firm, and Cynthia began the search for an attorney all over again.

In September, Cynthia received a notice requesting that she and Hector attend an interview together at the Chicago USCIS office. The purpose of the interview, called a "marriage fraud interview," was to verify that their marriage was in "good faith" before their family petition could be approved. Cynthia panicked. How could Hector attend an interview in Chicago when USCIS had ordered him to leave the country months before? And if he could not attend the interview, how could they prove their marriage was genuine? She called USCIS and was told by an agent to attend the interview alone. She did, bringing with her the letter mandating Hector's departure, as well as his airplane boarding pass. At USCIS's Chicago headquarters, Cynthia sat in a small office and answered questions about her and Hector's life together while an agent reviewed their file. "Do you know that Hector is ineligible for I-485?" The agent asked her. "Yes," she replied, "We do now."

In November, Cynthia received the approval notice for their family petition—Hector then became eligible for a visa. They began preparing for the next step, his interview in Juárez, and they navigated their case and their relationship in separate countries for the next year and a half.

Undocumented people and U.S. citizens get married to each other for all of the usual reasons: some combination of love, shared interests and values, readiness to start a family, and societal and familial pressures. Proof of immigration status is not required for a marriage certificate, and undocumented people do not face any particular barriers to marriage in the United States. In fact, immigration status alone does not inhibit the ability of undocumented people to attain many of the trappings associated with a normative middle-class U.S. lifestyle, including bank accounts, credit cards, car loans, and mortgages.

Still, for mixed-status newlyweds, disadvantages associated with undocumented status manifest themselves in both tangible and intangible ways. Unable to work legally, undocumented people typically earn less and are more likely to live in poverty than their documented counterparts (Mehta et al. 2002; Passel and Cohn 2009). Insofar as raising children and establishing a home require money, new families may feel constraints on their earnings more acutely than before. Moreover, starting a family with children raises the stakes of deportation by multiplying its effects, leaving children especially vulnerable to profoundly negative emotional consequences of forced family separation (Dreby 2012; Hagan et al. 2011).

Thus, mixed-status couples must negotiate all the challenges of marriage and family, such as figuring out how to get along, managing household responsibilities, and parenting children, in a context of heightened financial insecurity and fear of separation (Dreby 2015). In the process, gendered and legal inequities can become especially pronounced, straining relationships and affecting decisions surrounding

FIGURE 3.1   A U.S. citizen from Seattle visits her deported father in Mexico. Photograph by Steve Pavey, Hope in Focus Photography. www.stevepavey.com/.

immigration processing. When families do intend to go forward with immigration processing, gender and status differentially shape family members' relationships to the process and its burdens. This chapter considers the entanglements of gender and immigration status in mixed-status families and then explores the myriad factors that shape families' decisions whether to undertake immigration processing.

Gender, Family, and Status

As mixed-status family members participate in each other's lives, they share material items, like money, food, clothing, and housing, as well as immaterial matters, such as affection, pleasure, anger, disappointment, and fear. Immigration status is not independent of any of these; it permeates them all.

In intimate relationships, dimensions of citizenship and illegality commingle. U.S. citizens in mixed-status families can experience heightened anxiety and depression, constrained upward mobility, limited access to social and health-care services, vulnerability to family separation, and delayed long-term plans (Abrego and Menjívar 2011; Casteñeda and Melo 2014; Chavez 1988; Dreby 2012; Fix and Zimmerman 2001; Guelespe 2013; O'Leary and Sánchez 2011; Schmalzbauer 2014). For Cynthia, for example, anxiety surrounding Hector's status was twofold: she loves him and does not want him to be deported, and she also does not want his deportation to jeopardize her career. As Hector's partner, Cynthia was heavily invested in both the process and the outcome of Hector's consular processing case. She explained, "Yes, it was my husband, but it was my career and my future here. So it almost felt like it was my case, and it was my immigration status." The multiple strands of connection that exist between mixed-status couples bind them together, breaking through the apparent impermeability of legal categories in meaningful but incomplete ways.

Still, if the shared fate of family members blurs the boundaries of status, it does not erase them. Status distinctions can cause tension between family members, disrupt family relationships, and create or exacerbate inequalities and gendered exploitation within mixed-status households (Chavez 2008; Dreby 2015; Salcido and Adelman 2004; Zavella 2011). For couples that strive to achieve relative equality in their relationship, such as Cynthia and Hector, being mixed status means negotiating uneven burdens of responsibility. When only "legal" partners can drive lawfully, purchase insurance, open accounts, or travel safely, then those tasks will tend to fall disproportionately to them; as undocumented partners take on a reduced role in the household, they are subtly disempowered in relation to their lawful relatives.

Inequities related to immigration status also have complex ethnoracial and gendered dimensions. One Chicago-based study of undocumented workers found that, all else being equal—including occupation, education, U.S. work experience, and English-language proficiency—undocumented Latin Americans experienced statistically significant wage penalties for their immigration status, whereas undocumented Eastern Europeans (who are racialized as "white") did not (Mehta et al. 2002). And within Latino immigrant communities, gender, ethnic, and class differences heighten the marginalization of women, indigenous, and impoverished migrants (Fussel 2011; Holmes 2013; Stephen 2007). Notably, the Chicago study found that undocumented Latin American women fared the worst of all immigrant groups, both in unemployment rates and in wages earned, and the combination of undocumented status, Latin American origin, and female gender expression together increased the likelihood of unemployment by 220 percent (Mehta et al. 2002).

In fact, lawfully resident Latin American women experienced higher wage penalties than undocumented Latin American men, suggesting that, among Latin American immigrants, gender is a more significant constraint on upward mobility than immigration status (Mehta et al. 2002). In all, broader ethnoracial and gendered inequalities are not erased by immigration status so much as absorbed into it, connecting experiences of undocumented status to other structures of socioeconomic inequality.

Since undocumented people in general, and undocumented women in particular, are plagued by financial instability, their dependence on working family members is heightened and can exacerbate their vulnerability. Lourdes's story helps illustrate this complex relationship among financial insecurity, gendered vulnerability, and immigration status. Lourdes came to the United States with her mother and younger brother when she was a child. Lourdes's mother, who was a teacher in Mexico, struggled to find steady employment as an undocumented worker in Chicago, and the family lived in poverty for many years. Then, Lourdes's mother began a relationship with an undocumented man and eventually moved her family in with him. With two incomes, their financial stability improved markedly. But at 12 years old, Lourdes was sexually assaulted by her stepfather, and he regularly raped her over the next six years. Lourdes never told anyone, not even her mother, and she explained that she endured the abuse in silence for two main reasons. First, she was afraid that if she told her mom, her mom and stepfather would fight and her mother could be hurt. But also, she says that she knew that if she reported him, her stepfather would be deported, and her family would be plunged back into poverty. In Lourdes's case, her mother's financial insecurity, related to both her gender and her immigration status, heightened Lourdes's vulnerability to abuse.

Within mixed-status families, disproportionate rates of arrest, detention, and deportation of men undermine men's ability to financially and emotionally provision their families, with the potential to disrupt gendered family roles (Dreby 2015). Cynthia, for example, was conscious of Hector's disempowerment and tried to respect his independence by not opposing his wishes to drive—although she agonized when he did. She is not alone. Joanna Dreby (2015) found evidence that U.S.-citizen women with undocumented husbands conform more closely to gendered household expectations than undocumented women with undocumented husbands. Dreby suggests that U.S.-citizen women may be trying to compensate for their husbands' disempowerment vis-à-vis the state by bolstering gendered roles in the home. Together, this evidence suggests that state policies permeate mixed-status families, seeping into the ways in which family members navigate their intimate relationships.

Family-based immigration processing only intensifies the dependency of undocumented people on their lawfully resident partners by tying petitions for residency to U.S.-citizen or legally resident relatives. For example, Veronica came to the United States with a temporary visa to do community work for a binational (Mexico–U.S.) organization. She entered into a relationship with Francisco, a U.S. citizen, and after four years, they married and he filed a petition for Veronica's residency. That's when "strange things began happening," she says, and Francisco changed toward her. He could be sweet and kind one day and cruel or indifferent the next. He began seeing another woman and flaunted his infidelity in front of Veronica. When she demanded that he move out of their apartment, he threatened her. "I'm not going anywhere," Francisco replied. "Understand this: if I leave, immigration will follow you, and they will deport you, because your case is with me." Over the next two years, Francisco held the threat of immigration enforcement and the promise of legal status over Veronica's head, using it to keep her in the relationship. "My papers are my gold," he would gloat. Once, when Francisco threatened to call the attorney and have Veronica's visa petition closed, she told him that it was "not for [him] to decide" where and how she could live. But her words were empty, and they both knew it. With Veronica's visa petition in his hands, Francisco wielded nearly complete power to secure or deny her lawful status.

When undocumented women attain lawful status, getting "papers" can shift the gender dynamic of their relationships. For example, Gume, a Mexican woman in her sixties, said that attaining lawful residency has transformed her relationship with her abusive husband. "I'm not how I was before, timid, nervous, all of that," she told me, "Because I don't depend on him anymore. I have my driver license, I go where I want, I don't have to ask his permission." But above all, Gume says, now she feels able to call the police if her husband is violent toward her. She says, "Sometimes he would make fun of me, like 'Oh! I can't touch you because you're going to call the cops.' [I told him,] 'That's right. . . . They'll arrest you and if you get out and hit me again, I'll have you arrested again. You'll be in jail and I'll be in the grave. If that's how you want it, that's how it will be. You will not touch me again.'" With the fear of deportation lifted, Gume is empowered to stand up to her husband, even bringing in state authorities to help protect her, if necessary.

But existing research has also shown that gendered disparities may make it more difficult for undocumented women to legalize their status than men. In her research with people undertaking legalization through IRCA's 1986 amnesty provision, Jacqueline Hagan (1994) found that undocumented women faced a series of extra hurdles to legalization. In particular, undocumented women had less robust social capital, which provided an important source of information about the application process, and women were more likely to work in the informal sector and thus less able to produce proof of continuous residence since 1982, which IRCA required. Nearly two decades later, Salcido and Menjívar (2012) found evidence that women continue to face gendered barriers when they attempt to lawfully immigrate to the United States.

However, in the current period of mass detention and incarceration, greater policing of immigrant men may disproportionately encumber them when they attempt to change their immigration status. Men are many times more likely than women to be arrested for criminal and immigration violations and deported from the United States (Dreby 2015; Golash-Boza and Hondagneu-Sotelo 2013; Western 2006), and my research suggests that criminalization of men makes them more likely to have a criminal or immigration record that renders them ineligible for processing (Gomberg-Muñoz 2015). And as I explain in the next chapter, even men who are eligible for processing are often suspected of substance use, gang affiliation, and criminality by immigration agents who can deny their applications based on those suspicions. When I asked one Chicago-area attorney whether there were any factors that make it easier for some applicants to change their status than others, she immediately responded, "Gender. Gender. Women get it a lot easier. Women get the waivers quicker." She continued, "Until quite recently . . . any young man that went for their medical was treated as a drug abuser. . . . And in their medical exam [results] that they present to the consulate the next day, it says, 'This person is a drug abuser.'" In the current period, greater criminalization of men and greater financial insecurity of women create significant, but different, gendered barriers to legalization.

Deciding to Legalize

Given that undocumented status both constrains financial security and makes families vulnerable to forced separation, it should not be surprising that many mixed status couples seek to undertake immigration processing soon after their wedding. And with marriage to a U.S. citizen, undocumented people reach that first critical milestone on the road to legal status: they now can apply for a family-based visa. Still, despite the pervasive and profound insecurities associated with undocumented status, the decision to pursue legalization is not necessarily obvious or straightforward. In fact, although undocumented status is a source of repression and constraint, it can also be "strangely liberat[ing]" in that undocumented people are in certain ways outside of the system (Coutin 2000a). And for some undocumented people, the risks and costs of undertaking immigration processing are simply not worth it.

When I began this project, I reached out to Lily, a former student of mine who had once told me that she did not let her undocumented status be a defining part of her life. I was intrigued by her comment, and I wanted to talk with her more. Lily agreed to be interviewed, and I met her at her home on Chicago's southeast side, adjacent to expansive nature preserves. Although Lily had recently married Carl, a U.S. citizen, she said that she was not interested in trying to change her status. Instead, she explained, she is focusing on other things, like taking care of two younger siblings who had recently moved into her home. Lily said that she tries not to concentrate on the limitations of her status; instead, "I try to compare myself to people who don't have what I have, with people who are poorer than me, or . . . are worse off. . . . And when you take all that into consideration, for me being undocumented is not that big of a deal after all." Unfortunately for Lily, events beyond her control would disrupt her tranquility and, as I discuss below, force her into processing before my project's field season was over.

Even for those who aspire to lawful status, undertaking immigration processing can be a daunting prospect. Processing requires undocumented people to expose their presence to the U.S. government, register with immigration authorities, and have their fingerprints taken and their records run; for these reasons, immigration processing initially increases, not decreases, the risk of deportation (see Coutin 2000a, 110). Furthermore, consular processing forces undocumented people to leave the United States and automatically bars them from returning for 10 years; even those who are unlikely to be deported still run the risk of long-term separation from their U.S. families. As one woman, Kaitlin, explained, "Coming out of the shadows is what gets you in trouble. You can live under the wire. It's when you go to try to get legal, that's when you get the bar." And unlike deportation, which is a forced and unanticipated removal, consular processing involves deliberately and voluntarily removing yourself from the United States and separating yourself from your loved ones. Those considering consular processing must measure the risk against the potential benefits of lawful status and find it worthwhile to take the risk. This decision is not made lightly, and families must carefully consider several questions before they embark on immigration processing.

Do We Have the Right Kind of Family?

The family reunification system privileges some family configurations over others, limiting eligibility for a visa to select legally recognized family members of U.S. citizens and lawful residents (Boehm 2012; Enchautegui and Menjívar 2015). As I explained in the previous chapter, only applicants who have a U.S.-citizen spouse, parent, or child older than 21 are considered "immediate relatives" and become immediately eligible for family-based immigration. Everyone else must either wait in line, including "immediate relatives" of lawful residents, or be excluded from family-based immigration altogether.

Because the U.S. immigration system prioritizes "family reunification," it reproduces a certain ideal of "family," with attendant assumptions about gender, sexuality, age, and biological relatedness. Kinship configurations that fall outside this ideal are largely excluded from the family preference system. Kaitlin and her partner, Noe, for example, do not wish to legally marry; if they hold to this wish, Noe will never be eligible for a U.S. visa through Kaitlin. In another example, consider Luis, who came to the United States as a child with his mother. After several years of living in the United States undocumented, Luis's mother married a lawful resident and had two U.S.-citizen children with him. Luis's stepfather naturalized as a U.S. citizen so that he could petition for Luis's mother, who eventually gained lawful status through consular processing. By this time, Luis was already an adult and thus excluded from his mother's application. Now, because he "aged out" of his mother's application, Luis is the only member of his family who is undocumented. To make matters more complicated, at the time of my first interview with Luis, in 2011, there was also no pathway for him to change his status through a spouse because he identifies as gay.

Although identifying as gay or lesbian ceased to be a legal barrier to U.S. immigration by 1990, the U.S. federal government did not recognize same-sex marriage until 2013, leaving U.S. citizens unable to petition for their same-sex spouses. Then, in 2013, the Defense of Marriage Act was repealed, opening the legal possibility that people like Luis could marry a U.S. citizen and adjust through a spouse. The repeal of the Defense of Marriage Act is historic and a potential game-changer for thousands of people in same-sex, mixed-status relationships, but not, as it turns out, for Luis. By 2013, Luis had fallen in love with David, who, like him, had come to the United States without status as a child. Because both Luis and David are undocumented, even if they legally marry, neither will be able to petition for the other.

Indeed, the legal erasure of undocumented people in the United States means that no matter how many family members an applicant has in the United States, if those family members do not have the "right kind" of status themselves, they can neither file nor support an immigration application. Take Hector's family as an example. Hector's parents and siblings all reside in the United States with their spouses and children; yet because they are not U.S. citizens, none of them can petition for Hector, and he cannot petition for them. This makes Cynthia the only one of Hector's many relatives who can file a petition for his immigration, and it means that the rest of his family must be erased from her application. Their existence could actually be detrimental to Hector's case, despite the central role that their presence plays in Hector and Cynthia's everyday life.

This is not the only way in which immigration criteria can distort families' realities. Applicants can also move from one immigration category to another as they age or marry, and determinations about who is eligible for which category and when can seem arbitrary. For example, Abril came to the United States with her widowed mother when she was a child. Soon after their arrival, Abril's mother married a lawful permanent U.S. resident, and he filed a family petition for her based on their spousal relationship. Because Abril was a minor child, she was included in that petition, but the attorney handling their case erroneously told them that Abril was not eligible for a visa at the time. Years later, when Abril applied for DACA four months shy of her 21st birthday, an astute staff member at the legal clinic realized the mistake just in time. At 21, Abril would be considered a legal "adult" and would no longer qualify under her stepfather's application; with the clock ticking, clinic staff expedited her petition. Twelve days before her birthday, Abril had an interview with an immigration agent and was approved for lawful permanent U.S. residency. "I was saved by the bell," she recounted, "Oh, man. I could not believe it." If Abril had visited the legal clinic only two weeks later, she would have aged out of the original petition and become ineligible to change her status.

Although only select family relationships are recognized for the purpose of immigration, the categories of family members who can petition for undocumented relatives are further narrowed. U.S. citizens can file a petition for their spouses, parents, children, and siblings (lawful residents can petition for spouses and unmarried children but not for parents, siblings, or married children) who are abroad or in the United States lawfully on a temporary visa, but only U.S.-citizen parents and spouses (and in select cases, children older than 21) can petition for undocumented relatives.[1] Thus, undocumented people with pending family petitions through, say, a sibling, would be eligible for a visa if they had never entered the United States or lived here unlawfully, but become ineligible for the visa because they are undocumented.

If you find this confusing, you are not alone. Indeed, this system creates substantial confusion about who is and who is not eligible to legalize their status. Let us take Juan's case as an example. Juan is a factory worker on Chicago's south side who has lived in the United States since 1995. His sister adjusted her status to lawful resident through her husband and then naturalized as a U.S. citizen in 2008. She promptly filed a family petition for Juan. When Juan's visa does become available—the current wait time for Mexican siblings is 18 years, so he has some 12 years to wait still—he will have to go to Mexico to get it; there is no process for him to get a family-based visa through his sister in the United States. When he leaves, he will trigger a 10-year bar on his return. Because siblings cannot apply for a waiver of the bar, Juan will have to remain in Mexico for the full 10 years before he can return lawfully. In the current period, undocumented people without a U.S.-citizen spouse or parent have little chance of ever being able to change their status.

In all, as Deborah Boehm (2012) has pointed out, the family reunification system fails to treat families as a unit and instead creates a complex hierarchy of individual relationships and statuses that privileges some people and families over others. And the select few who have a qualifying relative have only reached the first step to lawful status. Many hopeful immigrants, and undocumented people in particular, find themselves ineligible to legalize their status regardless of their family relationships to U.S. citizens.

Are We Eligible?

Every week, new clients visit the legal clinic where I volunteer only to receive discouraging news: "No, sorry, there is nothing that you can do." Undocumented people who thought they might be eligible for immigration processing are summarily and unequivocally turned away on a regular basis. There is a profound mismatch between common perceptions of immigration processing and its more bleak reality.

U.S. immigration policy is both complex and opaque, and few nonexperts understand it well, including many immigration attorneys and federal agents, as well as immigrants and their family members. Because U.S. immigration law is complex and ever changing, getting accurate and reliable legal advice is a critical initial step. Unfortunately, getting good counsel can also be difficult. Immigration law is a highly specialized subsection of law, and legalization of the undocumented is a highly specialized subsection of immigration law. Not just any attorney will do. Even immigration attorneys who specialize in, say, employment visas for overseas immigrants may be poorly qualified to take on a consular processing case. To make matters worse, there are plenty of attorneys and notary publics who are only too eager to take advantage of hopeful immigrants. Notary publics, in particular, are known to exploit undocumented people by presenting themselves as capable of handling immigration cases (Mahler 1995), a claim that is facilitated by a misleading cognate—notarios in Latin America typically have legal training, and many are registered attorneys. In best case scenarios, unscrupulous attorneys and notaries take money for cases that have no hope of moving forward; in worst case scenarios, they send prospective immigrants with weak cases to consular interviews in their home countries, where they find themselves summarily barred from returning to the United States and separated from their U.S. family members.

Choosing a qualified and reputable attorney is essential because no two consular processing cases are alike. Even apparently minor variations between cases can make the difference between approval and denial. Take René as an example. René and Molly initiated the process in 2009 by filing a family petition, which was approved, but their case has been stalled at that first stage ever since. René's brother, Chuy, on the other hand, successfully attained lawful status following his marriage to a U.S. citizen in 2010. What was the difference between the brothers? Although they both entered the United States unlawfully, René entered twice and was caught at the border both times. Chuy entered once and was not caught. Although René has been here longer than his brother and has a U.S.-citizen wife and three U.S.-citizen children, he and Molly are still unable to go forward with their case. After Chuy attained lawful status, René and Molly even consulted with Chuy's attorney, hoping to get more encouraging legal counsel. But the attorneys agreed: at least for now, René's best option is to remain undocumented and hope that he does not get deported—although, ironically, being put in deportation proceedings could improve his and Molly's chances at legalization.

Because of these nuances, as well as the criminalization of migration and hopeful immigrants' need to prove their good moral character, details such as number, date, and nature of arrests are critically important. The first appointment with attorneys usually consists of a baffling list of apparently trivial questions: When did you first enter the United States? How did you enter the United States? How many times have you entered? What are the dates for each entry? How many times have you been caught? Did you sign any forms? Have you ever claimed to be a U.S. citizen, even on a job application? Have you ever been arrested within the United States? When and why? Each arrest, even for an infraction like driving without a license, is like so many marks on a chalkboard that, together, steadily decrease the likelihood of an approval. Attorneys must evaluate this record as a whole to assess the risk of moving forward with a case and the probability of success in the end.

Despite their critical importance to immigration processing, these questions can be difficult for applicants to answer accurately. Take René, again, as an example. René came to the United States 20 years

FIGURE **3.2** You could be deported! A sign at the legal clinic.

ago, returned to Mexico a little more than 12 years ago, and then reentered the United States. Thus, for René, he has come to the United States twice. But on both occasions he was caught at the border several times—he is not sure how many, but estimates eight or nine times in all. He thinks that all of these arrests resulted in a "catch-and-release" process that did not include a formal removal, but since Border Patrol agents did not explain what was happening to him, it is hard for him to know for sure. And knowing is critical. If René were to move forward with the next step in immigration processing, immigration agents would be likely to ask him about each and every arrest on the border, including the dates and outcomes of each. If René's descriptions of these arrests do not match DHS records exactly, immigration agents are likely to think that he is lying and punish him accordingly. For René, the point is all but moot, however, since a single arrest on the border after being in the United States unlawfully for a year is enough to earn him a permanent bar on reentry and a permanent separation from his wife and children—it is hard for him to think of a worse punishment than that.

For many couples, the decision to move forward is delayed until attorneys can run a fingerprint check and/or submit a Freedom of

Information Act request for DHS records. Until couples and their attorneys are absolutely sure what the applicant's record looks like, they cannot accurately assess the risk of processing. And even when immigration records come up "clean," there is a risk that the records held by immigration agents will include information that previous checks have missed. Thus, although René's fingerprints have been run twice and his record appears clean, his attorney still advises him and Molly not to risk consular processing.

A detailed history is important for another reason: sometimes it turns up details that help a case. In particular, applicants may have an obscure family petition that has been pending for several years and, if so, they may qualify for immigration benefits that they were unaware of. During intake sessions for DACA processing in 2012, for example, staff members at the legal clinic found several instances in which DACA applicants like Abril are actually eligible to apply for lawful residency.

Finally, families and their attorneys must consider whether U.S.-citizen or lawfully resident petitioners will be able to build a compelling case for their extreme hardship. As I explain in more depth in Chapter 5, extreme hardship is a subjective and moving target, but it must rise above the level of "normal" hardship that one would expect to result from a 10-year separation. This puts families who are largely healthy and financially stable at a disadvantage, since it may be more difficult for them to convince immigration agents that the petitioner's suffering during a family separation should be considered extreme.

Although eligibility to legalize begins with a qualifying family member, it also requires the ability to meet a host of other tests, including proving the immigrant's good moral character and the U.S. citizen's extreme hardship in the event of a 10-year separation. Initial consultations with attorneys thus involve a careful assessment of the family's entire history in the United States before a decision to move forward with processing can be made. In these early stages, another characteristic of mixed-status families becomes central to their decision to pursue legalization: their socioeconomic status.

Can We Afford It?

For the select families who have a strong case, one of the most significant hurdles that they face is cost. Mixed-status families often come away from initial legal consultations in a sort of sticker shock, unprepared for the massive expense that consular processing incurs. For some, the cost of legalization is simply out of the realm of possibility. Others must delay processing to save enough money. For families that do go forward, the expenses associated with immigration processing can accrue quickly and have a lasting impact on their financial security.

Some processing costs are relatively fixed and transparent, allowing couples to anticipate and budget for them. For example, applicants must submit USCIS filing fees for each form. As of 2014, the fee to file a family petition is $420. For undocumented people who entered with, and then overstayed, a temporary visa, filing an I-485 for adjustment of status costs $985. For undocumented people who entered unlawfully and then attempt consular processing, the hardship waiver fee is $585. The fee to run applicants' biometrics is $85. For successful cases, the fee to have the visa issued is $165. For unsuccessful cases, filing an appeal costs $630. All of these fees go into the coffers of federal agencies, either the Department of State or the DHS.

For undocumented people who overstayed a temporary visa and then adjust their status within the United States, filing fees constitute about a third of the direct costs for immigration processing. Attorney's fees, which range from $2,000 to $3,000, comprise most of the remainder. For undocumented people who entered unlawfully and must go through consular processing, attorney fees for the waiver packet alone averaged between $5,000 and $7,000 in the Chicago area during my fieldwork period. The lowest attorney fee that I encountered for a waiver packet was $1,500, charged by an immigration attorney who was just starting out. Cynthia and Hector paid $3,000 for their first attorney, which is relatively inexpensive, but the error that he made cost them many times over. When Cynthia and Hector changed attorneys, the cost went up dramatically; their new attorneys charged them $150 an hour for consultations and $15 per email to answer requests for information. The most expensive attorney fee that I came across was $10,000, paid by a couple in the Juárez Wives Club; other members of the group agreed that a $10,000 fee was higher than the norm. Although already a significant cost, this fee is only for the attorney to assemble an initial packet; legal fees for cases that require extra work or appeal can multiply considerably and last indefinitely.

Some couples try to reduce the cost by putting together the waiver packet themselves; this is risky, time-consuming, and arduous, but possible. One young woman in the Juárez Wives Club learned so much immigration law by putting together her husband's consular processing case that she later went to law school and became a licensed immigration attorney. Other couples seek help from nonprofit legal clinics, but the work involved in assembling a hardship waiver packet makes it cost-prohibitive for many community-based organizations. The Illinois Coalition for Immigrant and Refugee Rights provides a list of 14 nonprofit agencies in Chicago accredited by the Board of Immigration Appeals that provide legal services for immigrants; of these, only 4 do waiver packets, and then only a limited number per year.

As the process grinds on, the relatively stable expenses of filing and attorney fees are compounded by more variable, less predictable costs. After approval of the family petition, immigrants must travel to and from the U.S. consulate in their home country. In Cynthia and Hector's case, they purchased two airline tickets from Chicago to Ciudad Juárez, Mexico, and then two more tickets from Juárez to Mexico City, where Hector awaited the waiver decision with some extended relatives. Cynthia then flew back to Chicago, whereas Hector had to travel back and forth between the U.S. consulate in Juárez and Mexico City on two more occasions. Their final transportation cost was Hector's one-way ticket back to Chicago—the only one that they were happy to pay. All told, Cynthia and Hector spent close to $3,000 in airplane travel alone.

The hotels near the U.S. consulate in Ciudad Juárez, such as the Quality Inn and Best Western, charge about $45 for a night's stay. Most families do not remain longer than necessary in Ciudad Juárez and return to the undocumented spouse's hometown to wait while their case is processed. A prolonged stay in Mexico multiplies the cost of processing. Lucky couples have family members who will house them. Others must rent an apartment or room. Additional daily costs include food, local transportation, and miscellaneous expenses. And staying in Mexico incurs an indirect expense: lost income. Some couples only lose a month of income; others lose a year or more. Hector was in Mexico for 18 months and lost more than $50,000 in wages. Enrique was in Mexico for 6 months, setting him and Anya back about $20,000 in his lost income.

Since there is no reliable way to predict how long processing will take, there is no unfailing way to budget for it. Many applicants arrive in Mexico expecting to return to the United States fairly quickly, only to watch their cases stall and their savings dwindle. Some then seek work in Mexico. Enrique, for example, got a job in a pizza parlor to defray the costs of his living expenses in Mexico. Hector tried to find informal work in construction. But landing a good-paying job in

Mexico is not easy for most Mexican workers, and those who have lived in the United States for many years often no longer have the documents that prove their work eligibility in Mexico. And since their Mexican birth certificates and passports are tucked away in a file at a U.S. immigration office, they find themselves "illegal in our own country," as Enrique put it, which makes finding a job even harder.

While their cases are processed, U.S.-citizen spouses thus become de facto heads of households and often must support their spouses who are in Mexico. The longer processing takes, the more expensive this becomes. Anya and Enrique budgeted for a 3-month separation, and when their savings ran out, Anya took on a second job. So did Tanya, whose husband Marco was in Mexico for 18 months. Marco and Tanya and Anya and Enrique also racked up credit card debt, as did most of the couples that I interviewed. Cynthia moved back home with her parents to save money, and she and Hector watched their debt climb to the ceiling. One young woman, Beth, moved to Mexico with her husband, Jorge, in an effort to keep their household together while his case was processed. Jorge began working in hospitality and Beth found a job teaching English. But their income in Mexico was not enough to cover the filing fees and payments to their immigration attorney, and Beth eventually had to leave Jorge to resume working in the United States; she also took on a second job. In total, Beth estimates that they spent more than $30,000 on immigration processing—most of it paid for with credit cards. Marco and Tanya spent about $20,000 altogether. I asked Cynthia how much immigration processing has cost her and Hector. "I don't even want to think about it," she replied.

The high cost and uncertain duration of consular processing pushes it out of the reach of many working families; it is no coincidence that most of the mixed-status families profiled here have two incomes and are middle class. And even families who begin this process with a modicum of financial security will often go broke after years of filing fees, attorney costs, and interrupted income. Thus, intentionally or not, consular processing reproduces class criteria that have long been part of U.S. immigration policy: prospective immigrants must pay to play.

Is It Worth It?

If the financial costs of consular processing are prohibitive, then the emotional costs are even higher. Consular processing with a hardship waiver involves several layers of pressure, each one stressful enough by itself, which implicate all members of the family, including children. The work to put together a case is difficult, time-consuming, and expensive. And undertaking consular processing is uncertain; it requires families to separate without a clear idea of when they will see each other again. One Chicago-area immigration attorney said that she cautions new clients, "If you are going to embark on this, you have to prepare for a separation from your family. . . . I cannot guarantee that your case is going to be granted and or when it's going to be granted. And if you do this, if you start this, there is a possibility that you are going to be separated for ten years." This news can be hard to hear. New clients at the legal clinic are sometimes stunned that their options are so limited. "But I have been living here for years. Isn't there anything else that we can do?" they ask. "Nothing. Not unless the law changes," the legal clinic director tells them, passing flyers for upcoming events across his desk. "Go to the [immigrant rights] marches. And tell your U.S. citizen relatives to vote."

Families that take on consular processing must accept the risk of prolonged family separation or relocation. The stakes are high, and nothing is guaranteed—not the timeline, not the costs, not the outcome. This uncertainty takes an enormous emotional toll on families in the process, a toll that I discuss in more depth later. For some families, such as Lily and Carl or René and Molly, undertaking processing is simply not worth it.

When Immigration Processing Is Not a Choice

Many couples do not have the luxury of freely deciding whether to pursue processing, but are compelled to undertake it after contact with police or immigration authorities. For couples like Anya and Enrique, the expense of arrests following traffic stops, as well as the heightened fear that contact with police could result in deportation, pushes them to pursue processing when they might have otherwise waited. Other couples, including Lily and Carl and Jorge and Beth, find immigration processing forced on them by a deportation case. One attorney I spoke with estimated that about half of his clients were pushed into immigration processing by a deportation order. For these families, the stakes are even higher, the road to lawful status even bumpier, and the process even riskier. An in-depth analysis of the ramifications of deportation is outside the scope of this book (but see Brotherton and Barrios 2011; Coutin 2007; Golash-Boza 2015; Hagan et al. 2011; Kanstroom 2014), but in the final section of this chapter I share the stories of two couples, Lily and Carl and Beth and Jorge, to illustrate how a deportation case can affect immigration processing.

When I left Lily's home in the summer of 2011, she was largely uninterested in pursuing consular processing. But that December, when Lily and Carl took a vacation to spend Christmas with Carl's parents, their life was turned upside down. Lily and Carl decided to drive to Carl's parents' house in northern Michigan to avoid the risk of encountering immigration agents at the airport. But as they were driving near the U.S.–Canadian border, they were rerouted around a construction zone. Before they realized what was happening, they had crossed into Canada; when they turned around to go back, Lily was detained at the border. After seven hours, U.S. immigration agents released her to Carl, but they had put her under an order of deportation.

For the better part of a year, Lily and Carl fought the deportation. Their case had at least four significant advantages: first, Lily was already married to a U.S. citizen; second, she had no record of criminal or immigration violations; third, she was let out on bond, not put in a detention center, so she and Carl could take their time to fight the case; and fourth, they had enough money to hire a reputable and experienced attorney. Even the immigration agent who filed the deportation charges encouraged Lily to contest the case, telling her, "We have to open up this [deportation] case, but you don't have any record. You should be able to get a lawyer and go and fix your status." Lily's attorney requested that ICE administratively close Lily's case, which they ultimately did. Administrative closure means that ICE is declining to pursue her deportation, but it did not give Lily any status or any guarantee that her deportation will not be pursued in the future.

After that scare, Lily applied for and received DACA, which is a program for undocumented youth who arrived in the United States as children. DACA grants recipients a reprieve from deportation and a work permit as long as they maintain a clean record; it is good for two years, and when it expires, the recipient can reapply. DACA does not grant lawful status or make the youth who receive it eligible for lawful status in the future. Still, Lily feels a bit more secure now, which is especially important because her mother was arrested and put into deportation proceedings, leaving Lily responsible for the care of her two youngest siblings—both U.S. citizens by birth.

When I interviewed her for the last time in the summer of 2014, I asked Lily whether she ever plans to do consular processing with her husband. "Oh, sure," she replied, "[But] I don't want to do it now. . . . It would be nice to be able to apply without having to go through a whole process of going to Mexico and coming back, and now having the girls. That's mostly why I'm not applying for the I-130, because now that we have the girls, I need to stay here." Ironically, Lily's responsibility for her U.S.-citizen siblings makes her unable to risk becoming legal herself.

Jorge and Beth also undertook immigration processing as a result of a deportation order. In their case, Beth had surprised Jorge with tickets to see his favorite college football team: Syracuse. Nervous about driving over state lines, they decided to travel from Chicago to Syracuse, New York, on a Greyhound bus. One stop shy of their final destination, U.S. Customs and Border Protection agents boarded the bus and began asking passengers for proof of their citizenship status. Jorge told the agents that he was a Mexican citizen, and they requested to see his green card. He did not have one, and the agents took him into custody.

Jorge is fluent in English, and he passed his first night in detention translating for U.S. Customs and Border Protection agents as they questioned Spanish-speaking detainees. The agents bought him a pizza as a thank you, and Jorge was hopeful that they would soon release him on bond. Instead, they transferred Jorge to a detention center in Texas, and three weeks later he was deported to Mexico. It took Beth six years to get him back.

Because Beth and Jorge were not married at the time, they did not have a strong legal stance from which to fight the deportation. And once Jorge was deported, the stigma of his deportation cast a pall over their case and made it much more difficult for him to return. Following Jorge's deportation, Beth moved to Mexico and filed the paperwork for a fiancé visa. But when Jorge went to his immigration interview, he was barred from the United States for 10 years, and their petition to have the bar waived was denied twice. Although they now had a daughter and were struggling to survive in Mexico, immigration agents determined that Beth's hardship did not outweigh Jorge's "disrespect" for U.S. immigration laws. In total, immigration processing following Jorge's deportation cost Beth and Jorge 6 years and some $30,000. More important, it devastated their family, both financially and emotionally, and they are still working to put the pieces of their lives back together.

Immigration processing was even more burdensome for Beth and Jorge because Jorge's deportation undermined his credibility as a potential U.S. immigrant. As I described in Chapter 2, good moral character is a long-standing component of U.S. immigration and citizenship policies. In the current period, the ability of hopeful immigrants to demonstrate good moral character is eroded by criminalization and deportation. Indeed, for undocumented people, the approval of the family petition is just the beginning of their journey with consular processing. The second step involves persuading immigration agents that they are not criminals, but "good" people who are deserving of a U.S. visa. I explore that process in depth next.

CHAPTER 4

The Punishment

Marco and Tanya

As a 14 year old, Marco came to the United States with one goal in mind: to earn enough money to buy a motorcycle. In the fall of 1990, he left his home in Tlaxcala, Mexico, and traveled to the border city of Tijuana, just 25 miles south of San Diego, California. There, in a Tijuana bar, Marco struck up a conversation with a group of San Diegan teenagers who had come to Mexico to take advantage of the lower drinking age. The teenagers offered to take Marco across the U.S. border themselves. Marco, the son of a Polish farmer who had himself migrated to Mexico in the 1950s, "looks white," he says laughingly, and he pretended to be sleeping in the backseat while the teens drove through the border checkpoint. They then took Marco to the airport, where he caught a plane to join his older brother in Chicago.

At first, Marco had trouble finding a job because of his age, but before long the owners of a Polish restaurant "adopted" him, and he worked in exchange for food for two months before they added him to the payroll as a cook. Eventually, Marco was able to purchase his first motorcycle: a used Honda Magna. The bike was so big, and Marco still so small, that he could hardly ride it, but he loved it just the same. When he was 17, a car struck him while he was riding the motorcycle, seriously injuring him. Although the other driver was at fault, Marco received a ticket for driving without a license, and when he recovered from his injuries, he took his Mexican birth certificate to the Illinois

Department of Motor Vehicles to get a driver license. Three years later, he got a commercial driver license and began working as a local truck driver. On the weekends, Marco moonlighted as a DJ and go-go dancer in some of Chicago's most popular Latin-music clubs. With a steady income and plenty of friends, Marco partied away his twenties until he met Tanya in 2003.

Marco says that Tanya never asked him about his immigration status, but since he had a valid driver license, she assumed that he was lawfully resident. Six months into their relationship, Tanya became pregnant with their first child, and Marco worked up the courage to tell her about his status. Tanya was angry but agreed to try to make the relationship work. The following year, in 2005, Marco bought an engagement ring and proposed to Tanya at a family party. She accepted, and they got married in the summer of 2007.

In the years since Marco and Tanya first met, heightened immigration enforcement measures had eroded Marco's tenuous financial stability. When his driver license expired in 2006, Marco was unable to renew it. He lost his job as a truck driver and took a lower-paying job in a restaurant. The threat of deportation loomed larger than it ever had before. So when Marco and Tanya returned from their honeymoon, they consulted with an immigration attorney about the possibility of changing Marco's status. Marco had never been caught at the border, he had not left the United States since his first entry, and he had no criminal record. Their case was strong, the attorney said, "But you could be gone for one year or you could be gone for ten years. There is no guarantee," he added. Marco and Tanya went home to think it over. Eventually, they decided to risk the separation and move forward with immigration processing.

It took them a year to gather the documents and save enough money for processing. They filed their family petition in late 2008, and it was approved within months. They began to prepare for the second step: Marco's interview at the U.S. consulate in Ciudad Juárez, Mexico.

They decided that Marco would go to Mexico alone. This was a time of pervasive violence in Mexico, much of it concentrated near the U.S. border, and they did not want to take the baby there. Indeed, four months after Marco's arrival, three U.S. consulate workers were gunned down in Juárez, and the consulate itself was temporarily closed. Also, Tanya needed to stay in Chicago so that she could continue working to keep on top of their bills. Immigration processing had drained their savings, and Tanya's income would have to keep them afloat while Marco was away. At the last minute, Marco sold his work truck so that Tanya would have some extra cash while he was gone. In December 2009, he left the United States for the first time in almost 20 years.

Marco flew from Chicago to El Paso, Texas, and then took a taxi across the border to Ciudad Juárez. The taxi driver took him to a hotel near the U.S. consulate, where he checked in, and the hotel staff warned him not to venture outside unless it was absolutely necessary.

Marco's interview was scheduled for a Monday, and Marco arrived in Juárez the Wednesday before to complete his medical exam and biometrics check. Marco went to his medical exam on Thursday. There, clinic doctors took urine and blood samples, and they questioned him about his tattoos, as well as his alcohol and drug use. On Friday, he went to his biometrics appointment, where his fingerprints were taken and his face was photographed. Then, after a long and lonely weekend at the hotel, he got ready to attend his consular interview on Monday.

Marco took his file with all of his documents to the U.S. consulate at 8:00 on Monday morning. A long line had already formed outside. He made his way to the entrance and showed his appointment letter to a security guard standing outside. The guard let Marco into the building, where he went through security. A second guard gave him a number. After a receptionist checked Marco's file to make sure it was complete, Marco sat down and waited for his number to be called. When his number flashed on a screen above one of the service windows along the wall, Marco approached.

He stood at a long countertop facing an agent who was seated behind the window. The interview began. "When did you first enter the United States?" "I entered in November of 1990." "Why did you come?" "I came to visit my brother and to get a motorcycle. But I didn't go back and now I'm married. I would like to see if I can fix my status." "Okay, let me look at your papers. . . . Did you cross on this date in 2006?" "No." "Okay," said the officer, "Well, let me review your papers. Sit over there and we will call you again."

Marco returned to his seat in the waiting area. After about 15 minutes, the agent called him back to the window. "Okay, I looked at your file, and I'm going to give you a bar because you entered the United States illegally." He handed Marco a sheet of paper with a numbered list; the ninth item was circled: a 10-year bar for unlawful presence.

Dejected, Marco left the consulate and called Tanya. They consoled each other as best they could over the phone. Then, Tanya called the attorney. This is what we expected to happen, the attorney explained. And, actually, it was good news: the 10-year bar for unlawful presence can be waived. Marco would be given the chance to return home.

Around the time that Marco was attending his consular interview in Ciudad Juárez, Mexico, I went to Chicago's USCIS offices with Gio and Rosie. Gio came to the United States with his parents on a tourist visa when he was nine years old, and he lived in the United States unlawfully for 12 years before marrying Rosie, his high school sweetheart. Four months into their marriage, Gio and Rosie filed the paperwork to adjust Gio's status. Six months later, we sat in USCIS's cavernous beige waiting room in downtown Chicago; Gio and Rosie held hands and spoke in whispers while Gio, dressed in his best jeans, tapped his foot nervously on the carpet. Less than 30 minutes later, we were headed to lunch; Gio had been approved. In all, the process cost Gio and Rosie about $3,000 ("Worth every penny," Gio said) and took about six months to complete. Gio never left Chicago; he and Rosie were never separated.

The undocumented population of the United States is diverse, differing in almost every way imaginable; this variation differentially shapes people's ability to legalize their status. For undocumented people with U.S.-citizen spouses, there is one distinction that is arguably more important than all of the rest. For them, the path to lawful status bifurcates around one central question: how did you get here?

There are two main ways in which a person can become undocumented in the United States. The first way is to enter the United States without permission, like Marco did. This is most often achieved by the unlawful crossing of a border, but it also results when people misrepresent themselves as U.S. visa holders or U.S. citizens to immigration officials. People who enter the United States unlawfully, either surreptitiously or through fraud, comprise about half of the U.S. undocumented population. The other way to become undocumented is to enter lawfully—either on a temporary visa, such as a tourist or student visa, or from one of the nations exempted from visas   and then to stay past its expiration or otherwise violate the terms of entry. This is what Gio's family did. I will refer to people who enter lawfully and later become undocumented as visa overstayers; they comprise the other half of the U.S. undocumented population.[1]

Undocumented people are not equally likely to be either unlawful entrants or visa overstayers. Instead, these categories are tied to broader ethnoracial and class characteristics. In fact, many of the world's wealthiest nations—including most European countries, such as England, France, Germany, Sweden, Austria, the Netherlands, Finland, Greece, and Spain, as well as Australia and New Zealand and select Asian nations, including Japan, Taiwan, and South Korea—are part of the U.S. Visa Waiver Program (U.S. Department of State 2014). People from these countries do not need a visa to come to the United States. They can enter lawfully and stay up to 90 days without a visa; they are unlikely to ever be unlawful entrants.

For the rest of the world, whether a person can procure a temporary visa to visit the United States is often based on their "assets" in the home country. Ample assets are considered evidence that visitors will return home promptly after a visit, making middle-class and wealthy people more likely to be granted visas to visit the United States than poor and working-class people (Gerken 2013). For example, Anya explained the difficulty that Enrique's sister faced when she tried to get a tourist visa to visit her brother: "It is 2,500 pesos per person to get a passport, which is a lot for Mexico, and then $150 [U.S. dollars] each to get an appointment to maybe see if you can get a visa, and then if you get a visa, you have to have 10,000 pesos in the bank to make sure that you're not going to stay [in the U.S.]." These requirements push the possibility of getting a temporary visa out of reach for most working-class and impoverished Mexicans. And because of the history of migration between Latin America and the United States, coupled with their proximity and the likelihood that prospective Latin American immigrants will be working class, undocumented Latin Americans are more likely to be unlawful entrants than undocumented people from elsewhere in the world (Coutin 2000a; Pew Hispanic Center 2006).

As policies that grant admission disadvantage working-class Latin Americans, so too does the coupling of criminal law and immigration enforcement on the U.S.–Mexico border. Currently, unlawful *presence* in the United States is not a crime but a civil violation, and deportation is not considered a punishment but an administrative solution (Golash-Boza 2012b). But since 2005, the U.S. Border Patrol has been aggressively charging unlawful *entry* as a federal crime: a misdemeanor for the first crossing attempt and a felony charge for any additional attempts. Between 1992 and 2012, the number of federal convictions for unlawful reentry into the United States increased 28-fold, from 690 cases to 19,462.

By 2012, people convicted of unlawful reentry made up 26 percent of all sentenced federal offenders, and they served an average of 23 months in prison prior to deportation (Light et al. 2014).

In all, Latin Americans are more likely both to be unlawful entrants and to have immigration-related criminal convictions than other undocumented people. These two factors amount to a one-two punch that makes undocumented Latinos far less likely to be able to legalize their status, regardless of their family relations or length of residence in the United States.

The Legal Nonexistence of Unlawful Entrants

Gio and Marco's divergent paths to lawful status were forged by the 1996 IIRAIRA, which first established a legal distinction between undocumented people who enter unlawfully and those who enter the United States either with a temporary visa or from one of the nations exempted from visas and then overstay their departure date. IIRAIRA determined that visa overstayers had been lawfully "admitted" to the United States, whereas unlawful entrants had not. This distinction has important consequences for immigration processing.

First, to legalize their status, unlawful entrants must leave the country and apply to be admitted—as though they were never here (Immigrant Legal Resource Center 2012).[2] In contrast, because overstayers have been lawfully admitted, they do not have to leave and apply for admission; they can often adjust their status without separating from their U.S. families. Second, when unlawful entrants apply for admission, they must prove that they do not meet any "grounds of inadmissibility." Yet one ground of inadmissibility is a history of unlawful presence in the United States. Anyone who has lived in the United States unlawfully between 180 days and 1 year is barred from reentry for 3 years. Anyone who has lived in the United States unlawfully for more than 1 year is barred from reentry for 10 years. In Chicago's Mexican communities, the 10-year bar is known colloquially as "el castigo," or "the punishment." The bars on reentry are automatic and nondiscretionary—applied without regard to a person's length of residence, family ties, work history, criminal record, need, or any other consideration. Since these bars are triggered when a person leaves and applies to come back, they almost exclusively apply to undocumented unlawful entrants and not to visa overstayers.

Because Marco is married to Tanya, he is eligible for an immigrant visa. Since he had never legally entered the United States, he had to leave the United States to get it. Because he left and applied to come back, he was barred from returning. Because he was barred, he and Tanya had to apply for a waiver of the bar, a step that I discuss more in the next chapter. Together, this process cost Marco and Tanya more than $10,000 and left them separated for 18 months. Being an unlawful entrant pushes the cost and the risk of immigration processing to the ceiling, all but guaranteeing that many undocumented people will remain undocumented, even when they qualify for an immigrant visa.

Because unlawful presence following unlawful entry is a ground of inadmissibility, unlawful entrants can never meet the criteria for admission. When they go to their consular interviews, they already know that their applications for admission will be denied and their reentry prohibited for 3 or 10 years. Their task in Juárez is to avoid all other grounds of inadmissibility, so that they may be eligible to apply for a waiver of the bar and return home to their families.

Going to Juárez

Of the three main steps of consular processing—the family petition, the consular interview, and the hardship waiver packet—filing a family petition is both the easiest and the least risky, since it involves no commitment to move forward. Once the family petition is approved, couples receive a notice in the mail with the date of a consular interview in Ciudad Juárez. Going to Juárez marks a point of no return: once the undocumented family member leaves, there is no guarantee that he or she will be able to come back. Some couples suspend the process at this juncture, unable to cope with the prospect of indefinite separation.

The reality that the undocumented family member must leave and may or may not be able to return can hit hard. Families do everything they can beforehand to increase their chances of a speedy approval and prompt reunion. One woman, Pamela, explains how she and her husband, Victor, prepared for his interview:

> I was like, "You need to know my favorite drink. What's my this, what's my that? Where are my parents from?" He knew it, but he's not good under pressure. And he's not good with dates. He knows my birthday because it's the day after his. I kept drilling him, "What day did we get married?" And thank god, it's the same day we met,

so he knows that. The kids' birthdays, he gets those confused with other days, so we kept going over and over and over this. I booked him the hotel. I set up the transportation. Got him a little phone book in case his cellphone doesn't work. . . . We had heard all kinds of stories of certain people; they asked them for pictures, you know, that your marriage is legit. We were going through pictures. . . .

July 21st [the day Victor left], I got up, got lost going to the airport. I have been to the airport 100 million times. And he said to me the night before, he said, "Promise me you're not going to cry." And I said, "I can't promise you that I won't cry . . . but I will promise you that Security will not have to come and intervene. I will promise you that." And he said, "Okay, I'll take it." And we get [to the airport] and I said, "Are you going to cry?" And he said, "No, I'm not going to cry." He goes, "Why am I going to cry? I am coming home [back to you]. I am not going to cry. I am going to come home."

Like many couples, Victor and Pamela made the decision to split up, rather than go to Juárez together. Not only is a family trip more expensive, but also travel to Juárez can be dangerous. During my fieldwork period, Juárez had the dubious distinction of being one of the most dangerous cities in the world (Valdez 2014). Enrique described the area around the U.S. consulate in Juárez as "a war zone," replete with masked soldiers armed with machine guns. "You can feel the tension," Enrique explained, "You see that and you think, 'I want to go back to Chicago!'" Pamela remembers worrying, "All the shit is going down in Juárez, like all these murders every day. Now I am thinking, [Victor] is going to have papers, and he is going to die." Attorneys counsel clients to take extreme precautions during their stay in Juárez, warning them to travel by hotel shuttle instead of taxi, to avoid carrying cash or other valuable items, and to stay within the consular zone and never venture outside after dark.

With thousands of people visiting the U.S. consulate in Juárez each day, the consulate building is at the center of a microeconomy oriented toward consulate visitors. There are numerous hotels, a shopping mall, a Starbucks, and several fast-food venues near the consular area that cater to consulate employees and clients. There are also many dubious establishments, including legal offices that guarantee "100% approval" for consular processing cases, exorbitantly priced copy services, and "medical offices" that promise applicants a quick, cheap, and successful exam. The first test for people undertaking consular processing is simply to avoid all of the distraction and make it through their to-do list. In particular, USCIS sends them to Juárez to attend three appointments: a medical exam, a biometrics appointment, and a consular interview. At each appointment, applicants are screened for grounds of inadmissibility to the United States.

The Medical Exam

The first appointment is the medical exam. The medical exam must be completed at least two days prior to the date of the consular interview, so that consular officials will have the results by the time of the interview. There are two U.S. Department of State–approved medical offices in Juárez, both within easy walking distance of the U.S. consulate and nearby hotels. The purpose of the medical exam is to test the applicant for health-related grounds of inadmissibility.

On any given day, there are hundreds of people waiting to have their medical exam completed at one of the approved clinics. Applicants are given a number on arrival, and when their number is called, they proceed through a conveyor belt of different tests, all done by different doctors. First, they are photographed, then weighed, then they give a urine sample, then a blood sample, then they disrobe and are physically inspected. Finally, they are vaccinated. At each juncture, the doctor asks them questions. Some are health related, such as, "Have you ever had surgery?" And others are not: "Do you have tattoos? Have you ever been arrested?"

Clinic doctors are testing applicants for signs of four main grounds of inadmissibility. The first consists of communicable diseases, such as tuberculosis or sexually transmitted infections like syphilis or gonorrhea, which potentially present a public health risk. If detected, some of these diseases can be treated, and then the applicant can try again later. The second health-related ground of inadmissibility is a failure to prove vaccinations. Unless the applicant has an updated vaccination record at the ready, doctors at the clinics make rough determinations of which vaccinations they are likely to need and then administer them—each at an additional cost, of course. Third, doctors inspect applicants for signs of a mental or physical disorder that could pose a danger to themselves or others. Alcoholism, past institutionalization, and suicide attempts are all potential indicators of a mental disorder, and arrests for driving under the influence can raise a red flag for alcoholism. Finally, applicants are tested for drug use and addiction, the fourth health-related ground of inadmissibility.

Before the medical exam, attorneys warn their clients that if they admit to regular alcohol consumption or any past drug use at all, clinic doctors may refer them to a psychologist for further evaluation. At best, a visit to the clinic psychologist incurs additional time and cost; at worst, it can jeopardize a case. One attorney recounted an instance in which her client was coerced into admitting drug use by medical clinic staff. "[The client] was reduced to a blubbering mass and admitted that he had smoked pot three times in his life or something, which shouldn't be a bar. [He] was left crying and hysterical by this doctor and then psychologist. He admitted it after the doctor said, 'You know, we are taking your urine sample and if you have ever used any kind of drug in your life, it will show up here.' And he's like, 'Okay, I smoked pot three times.'" The client was hit with a bar for drug abuse, which is three years long and ineligible for a waiver.

Applicants may also be referred to the clinic psychologist if they have a criminal record to be evaluated for a "criminal" character. This is what happened to Alberto, who had lived in the United States since childhood and was arrested on assault charges following a street fight. Alberto went for consular processing after his marriage to Heather, and the clinic psychologist questioned Alberto about the fight and his subsequent arrest. When Alberto had a hard time remembering details of the event, the psychologist became angry, telling him, "Well, you don't remember. You don't remember. You don't remember, so I put down on my sheet that you're mentally retarded." Of course, mental disability also constitutes a ground of inadmissibility. When Alberto attended his consular interview two days later, the agent barred him from the United States and determined that he was ineligible to apply for a waiver. "We don't let criminals back into the United States," she told him.

Tattoos can also be a source of complication at medical exams, not because they present a health risk, but because they make a person suspect for gang affiliation. Savvy attorneys ask their clients about tattoos during intake meetings, and they advise them to cover or remove any tattoos that might invite suspicion. And because popular tattoos are often common among both gang members and non–gang members, all but the most innocuous tattoos can cause problems. For instance, people have been barred from the United States for tattoos depicting grim reapers, happy/sad theater masks, hands praying the rosary, and certain sayings, such as "my crazy life" (see also Jordan 2012).

Enrique has what he describes as a "tribal" tattoo, consisting of intertwining black lines, on his left bicep, which the doctor at his medical exam quizzed him about. Enrique recounted, "[The doctor] asked me, 'What does it mean?' I told him, 'Nothing. It's tribal.' 'Well, why did you get it?' [I told him] 'I liked it, and I wanted a tattoo, and I didn't know what to get, and I liked this and that's why I got it.'" Enrique laughed when he recounted this exchange, but the stakes of having a "suspicious" tattoo are high and can include a permanent bar for affiliation with organized crime (Jordan 2012). Pamela said that she thought Victor's grim reaper tattoo—the result of a lost bet with his brother—was "the bomb" when she was in her early twenties, but it turned out to be "not so nice" for their consular processing case. Victor had to cover the tattoo before he went for processing, at an additional cost of $500 for them. Now, because so many applicants have had their tattoos removed or covered, signs of a removed tattoo are also deemed suspicious and those applicants are subjected to additional questioning.

Finally, the expense of the medical exam can be a burden for families. The exact cost of the exam cannot be predicted beforehand, since the doctor determines which vaccinations are needed and charges accordingly; vaccines range in price from $30 to $95 each. Enrique and Anya tried to head off some of the cost by updating Enrique's vaccinations before he left, but to no avail: the doctor told him that he needed them again in Juárez. Also, many people have to do the exam more than once because their first exam expires before their cases are resolved. For example, when Nico went for processing, he and his wife Natalie already knew that he was going to be barred from returning to the United States for five years for failing to attend removal proceedings. Nico needed to have an exam done before his initial interview, and since the exam expires after six months, he would have to repeat the exam at the end of his five-year bar. Natalie, who was working two jobs to support their four children while Nico was away, complained about the $250 cost to her attorney. The attorney remarked that "[$250] is not a lot of money in the grand scheme of things." "I don't know about you," Natalie replied, "But I had to work a day and a half to make that money." For couples struggling to pay for processing, repeated and variable costs for the medical exam can be a significant burden.

After the exam, applicants return to the clinic on the following day to pick up the exam results. These are enclosed in a black plastic envelope, which must remain sealed and be handed unopened to a U.S. immigration official during the consular interview.

Biometrics

On their second day in Juárez, applicants attend their biometrics appointment, which must be completed at least one day prior to the consular interview. During the biometrics appointment, applicants' fingerprints and pictures are taken and then run through U.S. federal criminal and immigration databases. The purpose of the biometrics appointment is to check for grounds of inadmissibility related to criminal or immigration violations. The fingerprinting and photographing procedures are fairly straightforward, but the implications of these checks can be complex and life changing.

There are several grounds of inadmissibility related to criminal violations. Some are fairly obvious; for example, a conviction for terrorist activity, murder, or sexual assault will definitely make a person inadmissible to the United States. Yet even petty offenses—such as being under the influence of drugs or minor drug possession—can also make a person inadmissible. Some convictions that involve intentional violence, fraud, theft, or prostitution are likely to be considered crimes involving moral turpitude, or CIMTs, which have especially serious immigration consequences (Immigrant Legal Resource Center 2012). (Interestingly, working as a prostitute is a long-standing CIMT, whereas soliciting a prostitute is not.) For example, one young man, Beto, was convicted of two felony counts, grand theft and larceny, after he stole a purse from a car. Several years later, when he and his wife Christine attempted consular processing, those convictions were considered CIMTs and Beto was permanently barred from returning to the United States.

Other "criminal" grounds of inadmissibility are especially related to immigration violations and likely to cause problems for undocumented applicants. By itself, unlawful presence following unlawful entry is a ground of inadmissibility that applies to almost all unlawful entrants and is the reason why the bar on their admission must be waived before they can return. Other grounds of inadmissibility that can especially affect undocumented people include "alien smuggling," which covers everything from helping someone cross the border to sending money for a family member's passage, and "document fraud," or using false documents to enter or work in the United States.

One particularly punitive ground of inadmissibility is the "false claim" to U.S. citizenship. Any noncitizen who has ever claimed to be a U.S. citizen, even by checking a "U.S. citizen" box on a job application, can be penalized with a permanent bar on their reentry to the United States. This can even occur without an applicant's knowledge: one attorney explained that a few years ago Illinois Secretary of State employees were obligated to ask people applying for a driver license if they wanted to be registered to vote. If noncitizens answered "yes," they had made a false claim to U.S. citizenship that would get them permanently barred if they later tried to undertake immigration processing (or, if they were lawful residents, that would get them deported if they later applied to naturalize as U.S. citizens).

Some of these bars, such as the bar for unlawful presence and Beto's lifetime bar for criminal convictions, can be waived. Others, such as the bar for false claim to U.S. citizenship, cannot. One unwaivable bar that applies to many applicants from Central and South America is the 5-year bar for failing to attend removal proceedings. Until recently, Mexicans who were caught unlawfully entering the United States were typically taken back to Mexico immediately, whereas people from elsewhere in the world, but predominantly from Central and South America, were given a court date for removal hearings and released on bond. (Since 2004, the practice of releasing non-Mexicans on bond has been partially replaced by putting them in detention centers to await their deportation hearings.) Not surprisingly, many of those released on bond subsequently proceeded to their U.S. destinations and declined to appear in court. When they attempt to legalize their status, they often receive a 10-year bar for unlawful presence, which is waivable, and a 5-year bar for failing to attend court, which is not.

This is what happened to Paolo, a Brazilian man in his forties who was caught entering the United States unlawfully in 2005. When he was caught on the border, U.S. immigration officials first offered Paolo a deal: if he joined the U.S. military, he could get on a "fast track" to U.S. citizenship. But Paolo was nervous that the military did not pay well enough to allow him to cover his $10,000 debt to a coyote, and he declined. Then, he was given a court date in Arizona 12 months in the future and released. Paolo traveled to Chicago, where he joined his brother and found a job doing asbestos removal. He did not attend his court hearing. Five years later, in May 2010, he married Wendy. When they consulted with a lawyer about the possibility of changing Paolo's status, Paolo and Wendy were stunned to learn that his failure to appear in court would result in a 5-year unwaivable bar. Unable to face the prospect of a 5-year separation, Wendy and Paolo declined to pursue consular processing. In October of that year, ICE agents came to their apartment looking for Paolo's former roommate. The roommate was not there, but Paolo was. He was arrested and, a month later, deported to Brazil. Wendy then moved to Brazil to be with him, and they began looking into their legal options from there.

Finally, there is what is known as the "permanent bar." The permanent bar is applied to people who live in the United States for a year or more without authorization, leave, and then reenter the United States unlawfully. The permanent bar is waivable, but only after a 10-year wait period. This is the bar that would apply to René if he and Molly were to pursue consular processing. Not everyone is aware that they may be hit with a permanent bar, and the sudden and unexpected banishment can devastate a family.

For example, Ramón attained lawful permanent residency through IRCA in 1986 and married his wife Lupita in the 1990s; they later had three U.S.-citizen children together. Lupita was undocumented, but Ramón never filed a petition on her behalf because spouses of lawful permanent residents are subject to annual caps and can wait for many years for a visa to become available. In 2002, Lupita's mom became ill, and Lupita decided to visit her in Mexico. When her mom recovered, Lupita attempted to go back to her family in Chicago. She was caught by the U.S. Border Patrol and returned to Tijuana, Mexico, by bus. As she was unloaded from the bus, a U.S. agent whispered in Lupita's ear, "They are not checking trunks today." Lupita called Ramón, and Ramón drove to Tijuana to pick up his wife. She climbed into the trunk of their car, and Ramón drove through the border checkpoint and back into the United States. They picked up their children and went home to Chicago.

Several years later, after Ramón naturalized as a U.S. citizen, he and Lupita decided to pursue consular processing. Lupita attended her consular interview in June 2011. There, the U.S. immigration agent saw Lupita's record of unlawful entry and reentry, and he barred her from returning to the United States for 99 years.

When I visited Ramón in Chicago two months later, he was still in shock. "The boys cry for their mom every night," he told me, "especially the littlest one." The oldest boy had been literally sick with grief and had to be hospitalized for three days. To make matters worse, when

Ramón visited Lupita in Mexico, he was robbed and beaten. His shoulder was injured in the attack, and he had been unable to work since. "What am I supposed to do?" Ramón asked me as we sat in his kitchen, his three boys standing protectively around him. In 10 years, Ramón can apply to have the remainder of Lupita's bar waived, but they cannot wait 10 years for her to come home. The family could all move to Mexico, he suggested, but the situation in Mexico is bad. "*Está feo*," he said as he rubbed his sore shoulder. Anyway, "it's better for the children to be [in the United States] . . . they don't know anything about Mexico." Maybe Lupita could get a visa to visit Canada, Ramón proposed, and then try to enter the United States from there, where crossing is easier. But if she is caught, she could spend time in detention or prison and then be deported anyway. If all else fails, Ramón said, Lupita will have to cross the desert again. "The law makes people break it," he said. "We need her here. My children need her here." Soon after, Ramón's phone was disconnected and his house empty; I never did learn what he and Lupita decided to do.

The Consular Interview

The applicants' three-day trek in Juárez culminates in their interview with an immigration official at the U.S. consulate. There, all of the evidence will be put together and weighed by a U.S. immigration agent who will assess whether the applicant is admissible to the United States and, if not, will determine which bars to apply. It is a big day.

The U.S. consulate in Ciudad Juárez is not a single building, but a secured compound. As applicants approach, they join hundreds of other visitors standing in line, all clutching their files. The tension is palpable, Enrique explained, "Everyone is scared. . . . The people ahead of you and behind you are all asking, 'What happens next? What's going to happen?' Or, 'I heard this, I heard that. This guy was denied.'" He said, "All your fears start to rush forth and boil over. You don't know what's going to happen inside." The applicants must enter the consulate alone, since only people with appointments are allowed inside. The entrance to the consulate is kept clear by masked and armed security guards; family members wait on the other side of a covered fence and peer through gaps, hoping to get a glimpse of their loved ones as they come out with a decision.

Applicants first pass through a security building, where they are screened—no pens, cellphones, or other electronic devices are permitted.

FIGURE 4.1 Visa applicants wait to speak with an official at the U.S. consulate in Juárez. Photo by Joe Raedle/Newsmakers.

Then, they are given a number and told to proceed to a second building with a large waiting area and screens showing which numbers are currently being serviced. When their number appears on the screen, applicants approach a reception window, where an administrator checks that the file is complete. The file, now quite thick, should include the visa application, results from the medical exam, certified court dispositions, proof of income such as tax returns and pay stubs, birth and marriage certificates, passports, passport photos, and any other documents that USCIS or the Department of State has deemed relevant.

If the file is complete, applicants are given another number and sent to a second area. This is where they wait to speak with an immigration agent. When they are called, applicants walk to a long countertop, where consular officials who work for the U.S. Department of State sit behind glass on the other side. There, the interview begins.

According to my study participants, consular officials begin the interview by reviewing the file and asking selected questions from it. The questions start out easy: "What is your name? Where were you born? What is your spouse's name?" And then they move into more precarious territory: "When did you come to the United States? How many times? Have you ever been arrested? When and what for?" Officials compare verbal answers to written records, looking for hints of dishonesty; any deviation or uncertainty could invite suspicion. According to attorneys, officials may even try to trick applicants into admitting to additional violations by pretending to have evidence of border crossings or criminal convictions. Careful attorneys prepare their clients for this barrage in advance, so that applicants are not caught off guard. Of my participants, Enrique alone had a panic-inducing interview moment when the consular official asked him whether he had ever been arrested. In Spanish, Enrique replied, "Sí, por tráfico." "Tráfico?" the official asked. "Yes, just for driving without a license." "You mean 'tránsito,'" the official corrected him. "'Tránsito' is traffic, 'tráfico' means drug trafficking." Enrique was horrified by his error at the time, but laughs about it now that he is safely home in Chicago with his green card in hand.

Additional screens for inadmissibility not completed by the medical exam or biometrics check occur during the interview. One of the most important of these is the requirement that the applicant will not become a "public charge" or receive cash welfare or long-term care at government expense. You may remember from Chapter 2 that being likely to become a public charge is one of the longest standing grounds of inadmissibility in U.S. immigration statutes. Today, consular officials continue to pay special attention to applicants' ability to prove that they will not become a public charge (Immigrant Legal Resource Center 2012). The key piece of evidence for this is the "Affidavit of Support," a legally binding document in which the U.S.-citizen or legally resident petitioner promises to assume financial responsibility for the applicant for at least five years. The petitioner must demonstrate that his or her household income is at least 125 percent of the federal poverty level or secure a cosponsor. This form is supplemented by copies of tax returns and other proof of the petitioner's income. Consular officials may also look at characteristics such as the age, health, skill level, and education of the immigrant applicant to assess his or her likelihood of becoming a public charge (Immigrant Legal Resource Center 2012). Meeting the financial requirements to avoid this ground of inadmissibility can be a major burden on working-poor families seeking to lawfully reunite. This requirement also firmly ties a potential immigrant's admissibility to their capacity for work and their family's socioeconomic status in the United States.

In addition to the hard evidence contained in the file, consular officials will make subjective observations of the immigrant applicant. According to members of the Juárez Wives Club, an applicant's English proficiency, "clean-cut" appearance, and observance of middle-class norms during the interview may all help to persuade officials to approve a petition. In the end, all of this evidence, objective and subjective, is brought together in the final decision. Most of my participants' interviews were short and straightforward—between 5 and 15 minutes long. And at the end of their interviews, the official handed them a piece of paper with their decision.

"Criminal" Complications

Most people who make it to this step have clean criminal records or have only been arrested for minor offenses, such as driving without a license. There is good reason for this: undocumented people with serious criminal records are unlikely to pursue immigration processing because it will almost certainly result in a deportation and/or unwaivable bar. Some people, however, find themselves caught up in immigration and criminal proceedings at the same time. This is what happened to Alberto and Heather.

Alberto came to the United States when he was 12 years old, brought by his parents across the U.S.–Mexico border on foot. He met Heather through his sister, and they began dating when they were only 15 years old. At the age of 19, Alberto tried to stop a street fight that his brother was involved in; another young man was hurt in the incident, and both Alberto and his brother were arrested. While Alberto was being held in the local jail on probable cause, ICE agents came to pick him up. The criminal charges against Alberto were dropped, but he was compelled to sign a "voluntary departure" to avoid deportation. Heather posted his bail, and he was released into her custody. He had two months until the date of his mandatory departure, October 1, 2009, to prepare to leave the United States. Six days after his release, Heather discovered that she was pregnant.

They got married two weeks later and immediately filed a family petition. Soon after, the criminal charges against Alberto were reinstated, and a warrant was issued for his arrest. Heather and Alberto hired a criminal attorney, in addition to their immigration attorney, and he advised Alberto to turn himself in to police. But their immigration attorney told Alberto not to turn himself in, because if he missed his October 1 departure because he was in jail, his voluntary departure would turn into a deportation order. The immigration attorney filed a motion to extend the departure date to give Alberto some time to take care of the criminal matter. The motion was approved on October 1, but by the time they found out, Alberto had already boarded his plane to Mexico.

This is when their case "became so much more complicated," Heather explained. With Alberto in Mexico, Heather was reaching the late stages of her pregnancy alone when she found that USCIS refused to process their family petition because Alberto had an outstanding warrant for his arrest. They were in an impossible situation: Alberto could not come back to the United States until he resolved the criminal case, and he could not resolve the criminal case until he came back to the United States. Heather got in touch with her congressperson's office and persuaded them to intervene on her behalf; another year passed with no word, and then their family petition was finally approved. Alberto remained in Mexico, and Heather began raising their infant daughter by herself.

Alberto's consular interview was finally scheduled for May 2011. But when Alberto attended his interview, as I mention above, the consular official told Alberto that he was barred from the United States and could not submit a waiver petition because "We do not allow criminals back in the United States." The consular official then told Alberto that the only way to move forward with immigration processing was to purposefully get himself arrested in the United States. That way, he could be paroled into the United States to go through criminal proceedings for the assault charge; once that was over, he might be able to adjust his status. The next morning, Alberto walked across the Zaragoza Bridge, where he was arrested and taken into custody by Customs and Border Patrol agents. A week later, Cook County Sheriffs showed up to take Alberto back to Chicago in handcuffs and shackles.

Alberto remained in Cook County Jail while he awaited trial. There, he was found guilty of riot in the second degree, which is a felony but not a CIMT. Alberto was sentenced to 364 days in jail, but his sentence was stayed in favor of probation. Still, Alberto remained in jail for 14 more months, ineligible for release because of his immigration status.

With Alberto in jail and the criminal case resolved, Heather and their immigration attorney moved forward with the immigration case.

Because Alberto had been paroled into the United States and was thus lawfully admitted, he was eligible to adjust his status without leaving. However, immigration officials had lost the paperwork documenting Alberto's parole, and they charged him with illegal reentry—which would have triggered a permanent bar. When the attorney produced evidence of Alberto's parole, USCIS allowed them to continue with immigration processing from within the United States.

Heather and Alberto filed the adjustment of status application. But, in the end, their application was denied because the immigration adjudicator found that Alberto had committed a CIMT, "which is false," Heather says. A deportation order against Alberto was issued.

Out of money and unable to afford an appeal, Heather and Alberto made the decision to let Alberto be deported. With Alberto in Mexico, he and Heather initiated consular processing all over again, beginning with the family petition. As I write this, Alberto and Heather's daughter has just graduated from preschool, and Alberto has just attended his second consular interview in Juárez. There, immigration officials questioned Heather's ability to sponsor Alberto financially, but ultimately they decided to allow him to submit a waiver petition. It has been four years since his arrest; he has never lived with his wife and daughter.

For all undocumented people, the increasing criminalization of unauthorized migration has profound but uneven consequences. These consequences are most obvious in prolonged prison sentences, indefinite detention, and record-breaking deportation rates. But criminalization seeps into civil immigration processing as well, disproportionately burdening undocumented Latinos not only with criminal records, but also with indefinite and prolonged bars on reentry. It is ironic, in fact, that the bar for unlawful presence is called the punishment in Spanish, since U.S. law classifies the bar as civil, not criminal, and thus does not consider it punitive or "punishing" at all.

Heather and Alberto beg to differ. "[Alberto] is my *media naranja* [my other half]," Heather wrote me after our first interview. "I need him in a way I've never needed anyone else, and he understands me in a way no one else does." Years later, she is "stubbornly pushing to move forward . . . defiantly insisting that I be allowed to pursue happiness with my family." But whether Heather and Alberto will ever live together in the United States remains to be seen.

Outcomes

For some couples, like Lupita and Ramón, the consular processing journey ends at this juncture, truncated by an unwaivable bar on reentry. For many others, like Heather and Alberto, processing is postponed or dragged out indefinitely; their financial and emotional costs will continue to accrue. Other couples, such as Marco and Tanya, Cynthia and Hector, and Enrique and Anya, received the best possible outcome: a 10-year bar for unlawful presence. This bar can be waived, and it allows applicants to move on to the third and most difficult step of the process: the hardship waiver packet. Even for these "lucky" applicants, there are many months to go before they can return home.

CHAPTER 5

Extreme Hardship

Pamela and Victor

Pamela and Victor prepared for the consular interview as best they could. Pamela quizzed Victor about important dates and events in their lives; they prepped for questions about his entry to the United States as a teenager, his work history, and his family relations. They budgeted for months and built up their savings account. They explained to their oldest daughter that her daddy would be taking a trip to visit his mom in Mexico, and they assured her that he would be back soon. Pamela even joined an online forum for people doing consular processing with a hardship waiver so that they could keep track of how long the process was taking. Based on their attorney's information and the timeline posted on the forum, Pamela anticipated that Victor would be gone for a little more than a month.

The night before he left, Victor presented Pamela with a pendant of la Virgen de Guadalupe, an icon of Mexican Catholicism; he put the pendant on a chain and placed it around her neck. "Don't ever take it off, because la Virgen will take care of you," he said. "I know she will," Pamela replied, and she gave Victor her childhood rosary to take with him on his trip. The next day, Victor left for Juárez. It was July 2011.

Victor's medical exam was on a Friday, and his biometrics appointment was on Monday. He and Pamela spoke on the phone every day, and everything was going as planned; so far, so good. They expected the consular interview to go smoothly as well, since Victor had never been arrested or even caught crossing the border. On Tuesday, the day of his interview, Pamela told Victor that he should expect the consular officer to hand him a blue paper at the end—the blue paper meant they could apply to have his bar waived. But as he left his consular interview, Victor called Pamela in a panic. "Babe, get on that [online] group right now, my paper is white and it's all in English." "Shit, Victor, what did you do?" Pamela demanded, "You fucked up. You answered a question wrong." "No, no, no, don't get mad, because the guy said I qualify for the waiver . . . but it's a white piece of paper. I need you to calm down and double-check that white is okay." With Victor on the phone, Pamela checked the site: the white paper was the English translation of the blue paper. Victor and Pamela would be able to submit their waiver petition. Victor left Juárez and traveled to an aunt's house in Guadalajara to await the next step.

Their attorney scheduled Victor's waiver appointment for the earliest available date: September 5, 2011. In the meantime, Pamela and the attorney put the finishing touches on their waiver packet. In it, they presented evidence that Pamela would suffer extreme hardship in the event of a 10-year separation from Victor or, conversely, if she were to relocate to Mexico. The cornerstone of their hardship claim was that, as a nurse, Pamela depends on Victor for help caring for their children during her 12-hour and overnight shifts at the hospital. If Victor were to be gone for 10 years, Pamela would have to quit her job; she would lose her career and her house. In addition, Pamela takes care of her elderly parents—also a task that requires Victor's help. If Pamela were to relocate to Mexico, she would lose her career and be unable to care for her parents, all of which would constitute an extreme hardship for her. As a boon to their case, the United States was experiencing a shortage of nurses, and the attorney argued that forcing Pamela to relocate would not be in the country's best interests. On September 5, Victor returned to Juárez to submit the waiver petition, about the thickness of a city phone book, and then he went back to Guadalajara to wait.

September passed. Victor and Pamela talked on the phone every other day, but Pamela had no news on their case to report. September turned into October, and the weather in Chicago began to cool. As Halloween approached, Victor and Pamela's daughter told her father that she was getting her face painted like a butterfly for her Halloween costume. "Oh, yeah?" Victor told her.

"I am going to be home to see it." But Halloween came and went, and Victor remained in Mexico.

At the end of October, and with no word from DHS, Pamela decided to contact the National Visa Center to see whether they had any information on the status of their case. Operators at the center told Pamela that they had no information on her particular case and could not look into it until 10 months had passed since it was filed, but they did say that waivers were now taking an average of eight weeks to be processed. They would not, or could not, give her an explanation for the delay.

Pamela and Victor had budgeted for a two-month separation, and by the end of October their savings were nearly depleted. Pamela began picking up extra shifts at the hospital to try to keep their household afloat. "We had planned financially," she explained, "[Victor] had money for like four weeks, and then after that it was me supporting him. And I did whatever I had to do, working nights or working every weekend or working whatever [I could]." But the unanticipated and indefinite delay began to take a toll on Pamela's psychological health. Every day, she waited eagerly for news on their case, and every day she was disappointed. "October was the worst month," Pamela recalled. "The worst . . . I'm not crying in front of the kids, but I [did] cry every day."

Although Pamela tried to maintain a normal appearance in front of her children, they were affected by the stress as well. Pamela recalled an instance in which she was teasing her daughter during Victor's long absence: "I told her, 'I heard you snoring last night,' because she was snuggling in my bed with me. She would get in my bed with me because I was just so lonely. And she says, 'Yeah, mommy, I hear you every night.' And I go, 'What do you mean?' And she goes, 'I hear you crying for my papi every night.'" As November came to an end, their young son took his first steps, and Pamela began preparing for the family's annual Thanksgiving dinner. As usual, her extended family came over to celebrate Thanksgiving, and Victor's absence at the dinner table loomed especially large that night.

While Victor spun his wheels in Mexico, Pamela began calling the Visa Center every other day trying to get information on their case. "I thought, well, hell, I'm just going to call to see," she says. But she soon discovered that the information she received from center operators was not reliable. The main purpose of the operators, it seemed, was to tell her to continue to wait. Pamela explained, "[The operators] are reading a script. And the way the script is worded messes with your whole day. They tell you [that] you are . . . denied, or they tell you that they haven't made a decision on your case when you have the approval letter in your hand. . . . They tell you that it could be 18 more months. They really have no clue." Unable to get information from official sources, Pamela spent more time looking at online immigration forums. She had joined a site in which users put together a timeline of important dates in their consular processing cases, including their consular interview, waiver appointment, and waiver decision. Pamela realized that no one using the site had received a waiver decision from the Juárez consulate since September. She began communicating with several other U.S.-citizen wives whose husbands were also inexplicably stuck in Mexico waiting for a decision. They formed an online support group, the Juárez Wives Club. Within two weeks, the founding group of two dozen women grew to a membership of more than 500 couples.

Pamela and Victor, along with hundreds of other couples, continued to wait. At the end of November, one couple posted on the Juárez Wives Club site that they had gotten an approval notice in the mail. Similar posts quickly followed, and the mood on the site was celebratory. Buoyed by the news, Pamela waited eagerly for the mail every day.

But in early December, their daughter had her fourth birthday party without her father. Christmas approached. At a psychological low, Pamela decided that she would not celebrate Christmas without Victor. But when Pamela's mother came to visit, she intervened. "Don't be selfish," Pamela's mother told her. "You're going through a rough time, Victor is going through a rough time, but your kids don't have to pay for it. You need to keep this as normal as you can for them. You put up your Christmas tree. . . . You put up your decorations the way you do, you make Christmas cookies the way you do. . . . Just because you are hurting, they don't need to see that." With her mother's help, Pamela pulled herself together, and she and the children celebrated Christmas without Victor.

Two days after New Year's, Pamela was crying alone in her room when she decided to call the National Visa Center again. She recounted, "And I called, and Mr. So and So told me, 'Congratulations, your husband is in the system [his visa has been issued].' And I called Victor and I told him. . . . And he was crying on the phone when I called him. He said, 'Are you serious?' And

I said, 'Yeah.' And he said, 'Get online right now and see what flights are going out. And tell me what I need to have.'"

With Victor's medical exam and passport set to expire, Pamela booked Victor on the next flight from Guadalajara to Juárez. Victor would pick up his passport with the visa stamp there, saving the time it would take for it to be delivered by mail. Victor arrived at the Juárez consulate the next morning; he picked up his stamped passport from the biometrics office that afternoon. The date was Tuesday, January 4, 2012.

Pamela, their two children, and Pamela's parents were waiting for Victor when he stepped off the airplane in Chicago that night. Pamela recalled, "I took the kids right up to where they could walk, as far as they could go. And I saw him crying, just saw him crying. He only went with a backpack, because he said I'm not going to be there very long. And my daughter ran up to him and hugged him, but my son just turned around and walked away. He didn't know who he was." Victor was quiet as they walked to the car.

It was late as they drove home, and the two kids fell asleep in the backseat. As she drove, Pamela stole glances at her husband in the passenger seat. "I just couldn't believe he was in the car," she said. "I couldn't believe it, you know. I couldn't believe it."

For couples like Pamela and Victor, the third and final stage of immigration processing is the petition to have the 10-year bar for unlawful presence waived. A waiver of the bar means the undocumented family member can return home; a denial means at least 10 years outside the United States. To submit the waiver petition, applicants return to the consulate in Juárez once more to attend an appointment with a USCIS official. There, the official quizzes them once again about their marriage, work experiences, arrest records, and anything else they deem relevant. The applicant also hands over their hardship waiver petition. "Okay," the official says at the end of the 10- to 15-minute interview, "We will send you our answer in a few weeks."

The waiver petition that applicants drop off is a package containing hundreds of letters, records, forms, and pieces of evidence that, together, show that they meet two conditions. First, they have to prove that the U.S.-citizen or lawfully resident petitioner would suffer extreme hardship if forced to live apart from the undocumented relative or outside the United States for 10 years. What counts as extreme hardship is up to the discretion of the waiver adjudicator and can vary widely and unpredictably; however, it must be more severe than hardship that is a "reasonably anticipated consequence" of a 10-year family separation. That is, the pain and loss of being separated for 10 years is considered normal hardship, not extreme, and U.S.-citizen petitioners must show that their hardship is extraordinary in some legally recognized way.

Second, they must demonstrate the "good moral character" of the undocumented family member. The extreme hardship of the U.S. citizen is weighed alongside the character of the undocumented relative, such that the more extreme the hardship and the better the good moral character, the greater the likelihood that the waiver will be approved. If the evidence for hardship is not convincing and crystal clear, or if the applicant's good moral character is suspect, adjudicators will postpone the waiver decision and families will receive a Request for Additional Evidence, or "referral," that will delay their processing for several more months. Thus, having overwhelming evidence is key: Heather and Alberto's waiver packet, for example, was 736 pages long.

At this point in the process, the focus of a consular processing case shifts from the undocumented applicant to the U.S. citizen petitioner. This is because only the hardship of the U.S. citizen or lawfully resident petitioner counts for purposes of the waiver decision; hardships of undocumented family members and U.S.-citizen children are not considered legal grounds for a waiver. Insofar as the hardship waiver makes a legal exception to "the punishment" on the grounds of extreme suffering by a U.S. citizen, it is meant to uphold the value of U.S. citizenship. Yet the process causes a great irony: as U.S.-citizen spouses find themselves subject to the vagaries of immigration processing, they are shut out of the decision-making process, treated with cold indifference, and robbed of the ability to keep their families together. In this way, they experience immigration processing not as a celebration, but as a degradation of the value of their citizenship.

As U.S. citizens put together proof that they will suffer extreme hardship, they find that their actual experiences of hardship are distorted in at least three ways. First, the process discounts family separation as a source of extreme hardship; second, it compels family members to exploit their suffering for the purposes of immigration benefits; and third, it isolates the suffering of U.S.-citizen petitioners from the suffering of family members—including their own children. And although waiver packets warp families' actual hardship, it is not for lack of the real thing. Indeed, the expense, uncertainty, and indefinite separation associated with the hardship waiver process all but guarantee that families will experience real extreme hardship before it is all over.

Extreme Hardship

"Here is my file," Stephanie said as she sat down on the couch and placed the heavy plastic expandable folder in her lap. The folder contained hundreds of papers, carefully sectioned into two dozen plastic slots and organized according to different stages of the consular process. The first few slots held Stephanie and Javier's contract with the attorney and sample letters the attorney had provided them, along with receipts for the fees they had paid so far. Next was their approved family petition, the valuable document that recognizes their marriage as valid and makes Javier, as Stephanie's husband, eligible to apply for a green card. Third, Stephanie was compiling all of the information that Javier would need for his trip to Juárez; this part of the folder was relatively thin, since they had not reached that stage yet. Finally, the remainder of the folder was designated for evidence of Stephanie's

FIGURE 5.1 Stephanie's waiver file. Photo by author.

claims to extreme hardship. This section of the folder was also incomplete, but would eventually include Stephanie's hardship letter, letters from two dozen family members and friends with copies of their U.S. birth certificates or passports attached, her father's and grandmother's medical records, doctors' affidavits, a psychologist's evaluation, and a letter of apology from Javier. This file, their hardship waiver packet, was a labor of love for Stephanie—and also an overwhelming responsibility.

Knowledgeable attorneys advise families to begin working on hardship waiver packets several months in advance of the consular interview. Each family's packet is somewhat different, but in general, the packets have three main components. First, they contain letters from the "petitioner" and the "beneficiary"—that is, from the U.S.-citizen spouse and the undocumented spouse—that describe their relationship and lay out claims to extreme hardship and good moral character. Second, they contain evidence of the hardship, such as medical records, doctor's affidavits, financial records, bills, pay stubs, and tax forms. Third, they contain evidence of the undocumented person's good moral character, including letters from U.S.-citizen or lawfully resident friends and family members, church clergy, Little League coaches, employers, coworkers, and neighbors. Most packets will contain evidence of more than one claim to hardship in addition to evidence of good moral character. Generally speaking, the more evidence, the better; when they are complete, waiver packets are often several inches thick and must be transported in oversize manila envelopes or boxes.

Establishing the Relationship

After a summary and table of contents put together by the attorney, packets typically begin with letters from the U.S.-citizen and undocumented spouses. These letters paint a picture of the relationship and are organized around themes of great love, extreme dependence, profound vulnerability (on the part of the U.S. citizen), resilience and self-sacrifice (on the part of the immigrant), and a deep and unwavering desire to live in the United States. They often tell the story of how a couple met or grew to love one another and can begin to establish the good character of the undocumented spouse by describing him or her in moral terms, such as "kind," "generous," and "loving." The letters also establish the dependence of the U.S. citizen on his or her spouse, which lays important groundwork for the claim to hardship as a result of separation.

These letters often follow an established model, and attorneys say that they will spend several hours, even days, working with clients to craft compelling letters.

As they write their letters, U.S. citizen spouses must "exaggerate every little weakness," Anya explained, and often feel obliged to portray themselves and their relationship in ways that are unfamiliar, and even uncomfortable, to them. Cynthia, for example, said that she had to conceal her independence and self-sufficiency to emphasize her dependency on Hector. She said, "You're making yourself very vulnerable. And you also, I want to say, diminish yourself as someone who cannot survive without a husband." As U.S.-citizen women foreground themes of love, dependence, and family unity in their letters, they tap into deeply gendered ideologies about women's familial roles and values. Natalie, whose husband Nico was put in deportation proceedings following a trip to the grocery store, finds "[the letters] to be very syrupy sweet and quite distasteful, actually." Yet, deviation from the standard "syrupy sweet" model could arouse suspicion of self-reliance and weaken a case for extreme hardship, and attorneys push hard to have the letters conform to adjudicators' expectations.

After describing the relationship, the letters then move on to explain the U.S. citizen's claims to extreme hardship. And because immigration agents expect hardship to result when family members who love each other are forced to live apart, claims to *extreme* hardship must be grounded in something else.

Medical Hardship

According to attorneys, the strongest claims to extreme hardship often involve medical conditions suffered by the U.S.-citizen petitioner. Whenever an undocumented spouse is directly instrumental to the health and well-being of a disabled U.S.-citizen petitioner—because he or she provides the family's health insurance, or takes the spouse to medical appointments, or administers shots or medications—medical hardship can form the basis for an extreme hardship claim. For example, Anya's primary hardship claim was that she suffers from chronic cardiovascular problems that require ongoing treatment; this treatment is paid by Enrique's health insurance that he gets through work. If Enrique were to be barred for 10 years, Anya would not be able to afford her medical treatments and could suffer potentially disastrous consequences. Because medical problems are considered strong evidence of hardship, U.S.-citizen spouses can feel penalized for being too healthy. "How crazy is it," Kaitlin asked, "that if I had cancer, I would be able to be with [Noe]?" Because Kaitlin is not only healthy but also financially self-sufficient, she does not have a strong case for extreme hardship.

Sometimes, even when the petitioning spouse is healthy, another member of the family may suffer from a medical condition that can be used in the case. In these instances, the medical condition of the family member must be reframed as hardship suffered by the petitioner. For example, one couple, Guillermo and Marie, have two sons and a daughter; their daughter has a skin disorder. Because Marie works during the day and Guillermo in the evenings, Guillermo has been the primary person responsible for the child's medical care. For their waiver packet, Marie claimed that if Guillermo were barred for 10 years, she would have to quit her job to take her daughter to her medical treatments, resulting in an extreme hardship for Marie. In other words, Marie was compelled to exploit her daughter's condition to make a case for her own extreme hardship. "It's so screwed up," Marie said, "I was 'lucky' that my daughter was sick or I would not get to be with her dad." Ironically, immigration processing caused additional physical harm to Guillermo and Marie's children: their 7-year-old son stopped growing in the months that his father was away, an oddity that their pediatrician attributed to the stress of Guillermo's prolonged absence.

Amassing evidence of the sickness of loved ones can also strain family relationships. Grace, for example, takes care of her mother, who has diabetes. Grace's primary claim to hardship revolved around her need to care for her mother—a task that requires assistance from Grace's husband, who picks up their daughter from school while Grace attends medical appointments with her mother. Grace felt guilty using her mother's condition as her grounds for hardship and for compounding her mother's suffering by asking her to get letters from her doctors that testified to her illness—a task that her mother was reluctant to do.

The reluctance of Grace's mother to discuss her son-in-law's immigration case with her physicians is understandable: doctors and nurses may or may not be sympathetic or inclined to help an undocumented person, and having to disclose immigration woes can be a source of discomfort. Yet letters from physicians are crucial to establishing medical hardship because the word of family members is not considered sufficient. In fact, notices from USCIS emphasize that claims to hardship should be "supported by documentary evidence; merely stating that your U.S. citizen spouse or parent would suffer extreme hardship is not sufficient. . . . Claims of hardship due to medical or health concerns should be supported by a medical or healthcare professional's statement." To make a strong case for medical hardship, packets include doctor's affidavits, hospital bills, results from blood tests, x-rays, cardiograms, ultrasounds, and even copies of prescriptions. This "hard evidence" is further supplemented by letters from friends and relatives who can describe the role that the undocumented family member plays in taking care of the sick or disabled U.S. citizen or his or her close relative.

The task of amassing these letters from family members can be burdensome and create tension between U.S.-citizen petitioners and their relatives. After Stephanie and Javier's initial consultation with an attorney, for example, Stephanie worried about asking her family members to help with their waiver petition. She explained:

> When we met our attorney and she asked . . . me questions about my family, I was so hesitant to answer her questions, because me and my family don't have the best relationship. . . . She said, "I need 20 pictures of Javier with your family." And I was like, how am I going to do that? We're not that type of family. I left the [attorney's] office, and I had a million things going through my head. She asked about my dad and my grandma, they both have diabetes; my dad has a problem with his pancreas. So she asked me about their health and [told me to get] all their medical records and their letters.
>
> [Shortly afterward] my sister had a barbecue, and that was one of the last times my family was going to be together before my brother left for the military. So I felt torn by that, because we're supposed to be focusing on my brother, and here I am like, can you help us, too?
>
> So I copied the sample [letter] from the attorney, and [my dad and grandma] were fine with that, but when they started to write their letters, they had questions like, "Why do they need to know that I was born in the United States? Obviously I was born in the United States. Why do they need to know where I live?" They were offended by it. "This is supposed to be about Javier, why do they need all this information about me?"
>
> And you could tell that they were getting frustrated when I told them, you have to put this in, or take this out. Like my grandma has

to rewrite her letter, but I'm so hesitant to tell her because she has been so irritated. I had to ask her for her medical records, "Why do they need my medical records? How many medical records do they need? Why don't your lawyers get the medical records, why do I have to go do it?" My dad has no idea where his birth certificate is, "Why do they need my birth certificate? Here is a copy of my driver license." It's like pulling teeth with my dad, because I'm going to have to go to his house to make sure that he does it, so I can get what I need. And they have to pay for it, too, so I'm telling them, "Don't worry about it, I'll pay for it." And that's another expense, too.

So, my family, they all have their own lives and their own things to do, and I feel like I'm behind them, pushing them to do this. And they don't understand why I need these things and why I'm acting like I am.

The importance of medical hardship to a waiver case puts pressure on U.S. citizens to exploit their own health problems and those of their family members. As U.S. citizens struggle to put together a strong case and increase the chances of their spouse's approval, they may compromise their relationships with other family members, who may not understand or approve of the requirements for proving extreme hardship.

Financial Hardship

Waiver adjudicators also consider severe financial decline as evidence of extreme hardship. Financial hardship must go above and beyond simple loss of income, which is expected and therefore regular, not extreme, and involve a profound degradation in the lifestyle of the U.S.-citizen petitioner, such as the loss of a house or career. As with medical hardship, claims to financial hardship must be well documented with hard evidence, including monthly bills, receipts, canceled rent checks, car notes, tax forms, and pay stubs that go back for months or years.

Documenting the potential for financial decline is easiest if the undocumented spouse has a high income that the U.S.-citizen spouse relies on. U.S. citizens with middle-class incomes may be penalized if they are too financially self-sufficient. This involves an especially tricky balancing act for them, since petitioning spouses must also demonstrate that their household income is at least 125 percent of the federal poverty level to qualify their spouse for a visa. Thus, to demonstrate financial hardship, petitioning spouses must make enough to qualify for immigration processing but not enough to be financially secure without their spouses. For example, Beth and Jorge's waiver petition was denied twice when immigration adjudicators determined that Beth, who is a high school teacher, was financially secure and would not suffer extreme hardship without Jorge's income.

In some cases, U.S.-citizen spouses may be able to show that they would lose their career if their spouse's bar is not waived. For example, in her letter, Anya claimed, "If I had to move to Mexico, imagine how painful that would be for me because here I am, American educated, invested all this money in my career, and I have to waste it because that's not going to be useful for me in Mexico." Cynthia also used her education and medical training as her primary claim to hardship, arguing that her medical career would be thrown away if Hector were barred. Similarly, Pamela was able to show that, without Victor, she would lose her job as a nurse. Interestingly, Anya's, Cynthia's, and Pamela's waiver petitions were all approved on the first try.

Working-poor families may have the hardest time showing that financial decline should be considered extreme. For example, Jane was employed in a fast-food restaurant when she petitioned for her husband, Isaiah, who worked at the restaurant with her. The waiver adjudicator determined that Jane's claim to financial hardship was not extreme because the loss of Isaiah's modest income was not enough to substantially degrade Jane's living conditions. Moreover, the adjudicator decided that Jane, who does not speak Spanish and had never set foot in Mexico before, did not earn enough herself to make moving to Mexico a hardship for her. Their waiver petition was referred until Jane could provide more compelling evidence of her hardship.

Emotional Hardship

Waiver adjudicators expect that families who are separated will suffer emotional hardship, and emotional suffering itself is not a strong claim to extreme hardship. According to attorneys, the yardstick for proving extreme emotional hardship has moved over the years—as more and more U.S.-citizen petitioners based their hardship claims on separation anxiety and depression, those conditions came to be considered regular and no longer extreme. Now, strong claims to emotional hardship must be supported by evidence of a preexisting mental disorder that would be triggered or worsened by a 10-year separation. Of course, a claim like this must be supported by a psychologist's affidavit, prescriptions for psychotropic drugs, and any other available evidence.

None of my interviewees used emotional hardship as his or her primary claim, but many sought psychological evaluation at the advice of their attorneys as a supplement to their primary hardship claims. Anya and Cynthia, for example, both obtained affidavits from a psychologist attesting to their separation anxiety; this was used in conjunction with their claims to medical and financial hardship to support the waiver petition.

Relocation Hardship

Not only must U.S.-citizen petitioners make a compelling case that they cannot survive without their immigrant spouses, but also they must degrade their spouses' places of origin to show that they cannot live there either. That is, they must show that relocating to their spouse's native country would constitute an extreme hardship for them.

For petitioners with Mexican-origin spouses, this often means reproducing stereotypes of Mexico as an impoverished and violence-ridden backwater. Anya said that she was advised to emphasize her fear of being targeted for violence in Mexico because of her "Anglo" appearance, capitalizing on racist stereotypes of dangerous Latin American men. Or consider the case of Jane and Isaiah, whose waiver was referred until Jane could provide more evidence that moving to Mexico would constitute extreme hardship for her. To boost their case, Jane's attorney asked for photographic proof of how difficult life is in Mexico. Jane bought a camera and sent it to Isaiah with instructions to take pictures showing poverty in his hometown in Puebla. He sent back photos of flowers and parks, and their waiver petition was denied.

As Stephanie and Jane's cases show, the focus on U.S. citizens places the brunt of responsibility for a waiver petition on them—a situation with the potential to cause additional strain on relationships. For example, Isaiah's unwillingness to demean his home made Jane resentful and angry. She implored him, "You can't even take a picture of, like, something that looks bad—you're giving me a pretty little manicured gazebo and a garden?" As their case dragged on, Jane grew increasingly frustrated. "It felt like almost every time that we were talking, we were fighting, fighting, fighting." After their waiver petition was denied, Jane moved to Mexico to live out the 10-year bar with Isaiah there.

In all, standards for extreme hardship both exploit and grossly distort families' actual experiences of hardship. They reify complex and
multifaceted human needs as medical or financial "problems" with veri-
fiable "solutions." They also deny undocumented people and children
any claims to hardship, isolating U.S.-citizen petitioners from their
actual relationships, experiences, wants, and needs and reducing them
to a citizenship status and hardship claim. And because the stress associated with putting together a waiver packet can strain family relationships, the process actually creates hardship where it did not exist before.

Good Moral Character

The final component of the petitioner and beneficiary letters consists of
an apology for having violated U.S. immigration law and a plea to
waive the bar. This "mea culpa" is not just an afterthought—it amounts
to a compulsory acknowledgment that U.S. immigration law is legitimate and any violation of the law is the fault of offending immigrants.
"Accepting" personal responsibility for having violated the law is an
essential part of establishing the good moral character of the undocumented applicant—the second important component of a hardship
waiver packet.

For undocumented people, the claim to good moral character is
already in doubt—tarnished by undocumented status and the violation
of immigration policy that it implies. Because the yardstick of good
moral character is devised largely in opposition to "criminality," it
moves ever further out of reach for people with repeat immigration
violations or arrest records in the United States. Convictions for some
crimes, such as CIMT, prevent the undocumented person from ever
being able to establish good moral character. In those cases, waiver petitions are unlikely to be approved even with strong claims to extreme
hardship.

Clean criminal and immigration records are key to establishing
good moral character, but other characteristics are considered indicative
of good character as well. In particular, adjudicators consider the undocumented person's assimilation into U.S. society and involvement in their
community evidence of good moral character. To establish community
integration, applicants collect dozens of letters from family members and
friends, coworkers, neighbors, church clergy and parishioners, and other
members of the community who can speak to the family relationship,

hardship claim, and the undocumented person's character. Notably, all of these letters must be written and signed by U.S. citizens or lawful permanent residents; proof of their legal status must be attached to each letter. Letters from undocumented people are not considered and could even hurt a case.

Additional evidence of assimilation can come from educational institutions, and families include copies of degrees, diplomas, certificates, and school transcripts earned by the undocumented applicant. In particular, evidence that the applicant has been studying English is considered evidence of good character. Families can also get letters from applicants' employers—when they are willing—that speak to the reliability and work ethic of the undocumented person.

In all, the more the undocumented person has been able to avoid encounters with immigration and police authorities and the more tightly they can conform to middle-class U.S. norms such as English language abilities and a consistent, long-term employment record, the stronger their case for good moral character.

Waiting for a Decision

The opacity of the process, uncertainty, cost, and difficulty putting together a case combine to create profound emotional strain on families undertaking processing. This strain comes to a head during the wait for waiver decisions, when spouses are separated indefinitely. Pamela says that being away from Victor "was just awful. It was awful. You feel like a part of you is just ripped out, and then you hear them so far away, and they feel the same way." The anxiety surrounding immigration processing can consume a relationship. Beth says that she and Jorge "were so focused on immigration, and that was the main thing that we talked about and thought about. . . . It's like if you focus on that, then you're not focusing on the love and the good stuff."

During the period of separation, U.S. citizens become heads of households and single parents and often must support their spouses abroad—a situation with the potential to undermine household roles and create bitterness and resentment. For example, Grace and Carlos were separated for six months when Carlos underwent consular processing. While he was gone, Grace took care of their toddler, managed their immigration case, worked full-time, and, to her surprise and dismay, gave birth to their second child before he came home. The stress of that experience was so great that Grace says, "Sometimes I feel like [my husband] should feel guilty because I was here. . . . I went through all this, and sometimes I don't feel like he appreciates everything that I did."

For U.S. citizens like Grace, the stress of keeping a household together is often compounded by the stress of taking responsibility for the immigration case. For example, Cynthia chose her and Hector's attorney, and she was the one who took the fall when the attorney erred and Hector was prematurely expelled from the United States. Hector's resentment and Cynthia's guilt grew when Cynthia could not get any information from immigration agencies about why their case was taking so long to process. "Hector was just really upset and we would fight a lot," Cynthia recalled. "He was frustrated, and he kept insisting that I talk to the lawyer, but the lawyers couldn't tell me anything. And every email that I would send would cost me 15 dollars. . . . He wouldn't accuse me of being incompetent or anything like that, but I think his comments about how the lawyers weren't working hard enough, or, like, 'Why don't you ask them?' that made me feel like he was . . . indirectly blaming me for it, and I felt a lot of guilt." While Jane gathered evidence for her and Isaiah's waiver packet, she said, "I would get so angry, every time he messed up, because I felt like it was all on me; I'm running back and forth from the lawyer; I'm going to people, having them write letters, proofreading the letters, helping them figure this stuff out. I'm saving the money, I'm working, I'm doing all this." Politically, the sole focus on U.S. citizens' hardship is meant to elevate the status of U.S. citizenship, but it also burdens U.S.-citizen spouses with the brunt of work and responsibility for a profoundly demanding process.

For their part, undocumented spouses are banished from their homes with little influence over the case or the future of their families. If consular processing makes U.S. citizens bear a disproportionate burden of the work, then it further disempowers undocumented spouses. When Enrique left for Mexico, he says that at first he was excited to visit with family members whom he had not seen in 14 years. He was especially happy to see his cousin, who agreed to let Enrique stay at her house. But when his short visit became indefinitely extended, Enrique began to feel like an intruder. He became morose and depressed and spent his days staring at the television. As the months dragged on, Enrique began to doubt the decision to undertake processing in the first place. He explained, "That's when my positivity began to turn negative, and you can't see things positively anymore. You begin to think that maybe you made a mistake. Maybe trying to get legal was a mistake, and you shouldn't have done it. Because now you're away from the person you love. You're away from your family." At a low point, he and Anya began fighting every time they talked on the phone. "We were so stressed out," he recalled. "She didn't understand what I was going through, and I didn't understand what she was going through." Eventually, Enrique lost hope in a quick return and decided to try to find work in Mexico; he got a job in a pizzeria and moved from his cousin's home into a one-room apartment. Five months into his wait, Enrique was surfing the Internet when he saw that a Juárez Wives Club couple had been approved—it was the first approval in three months. Alone in his apartment, he cried with relief.

After months of waiting in Mexico while his wife worked two jobs to support the family in Chicago, Marco began making desperate plans to come home. He said to himself, "I'm going to have to go back like everyone else, with a coyote. What should I do? Should I wait or should I go back? I have my family [there]. They force you to make a drastic decision." After 6 months, Marco and Tanya found out they had been referred, and they had to provide additional evidence of Tanya's hardship. Tanya rewrote her letter emphasizing the hardship that she was experiencing working two jobs and parenting their daughter alone while Marco was away. She also got additional letters from family members and friends, and she sought psychological counseling to document the emotional toll that Marco's absence was taking on her. Another year later, their hardship waiver was finally approved. Marco came home to his wife and daughter after an 18-month absence, although, as you will see, his troubles with immigration were not over yet.

The Wheels Come Off in Juárez

The decision to grant, refer, or deny a waiver rests with an individual adjudicator who has complete discretion in his or her decision. Since the definition of extreme hardship is not fixed or standardized and can turn into regular hardship when it becomes common, extreme hardship is a moving and unpredictable target. Together, discretion and shifting standards make the waiver process profoundly uncertain—even families that have strong claims to hardship can be denied waivers in the end. One attorney explained, "I used to tell clients that if they had kids and there were no complicating factors, like criminal convictions or prior issues with immigration, it was pretty likely that they would get approved on the quicker track [i.e., not referred]. . . . But then I started getting all these referrals." The only way for attorneys to know which hardship claims are compelling at any given time is to send clients for processing and assess who gets approved and who does not. Sometimes they can detect trends in decision making, but other times, the attorney added, "There is no rhyme or reason to who gets referred and who gets approved immediately."

This uncertainty is compounded by the knowledge that their future together rests entirely in the hands of a nameless and faceless adjudicator—a person whom they will never meet. The imbalance of knowledge and power can be profoundly unsettling. "You have no idea who is making these decisions. You can't face the person," Beth explained. "You can't even read who signs the letter. . . . That has always bothered me, because I feel like, if someone's doing this to me and my family, I want to know their name. I don't want them to be hiding behind this veil of bureaucracy [where they] have this power to destroy someone's life and not even tell you who they are." Grace lamented, "It's just amazing how someone has that much power. Whoever is reviewing has that much power to say, 'Yes, your family can be together . . . [or] you're fine by yourself. You don't need him.'" U.S.-citizen spouses like Grace and Beth are never interviewed by waiver adjudicators; they are not even allowed to enter the consulate with their husbands. As they submit to this process, U.S. citizens turn over control of their lives to an adjudicator and lose the power to make decisions about their own and their families' well-being.

The lack of consistency and transparency in waiver adjudication can make the process feel like a game with rules that only adjudicators know. One attorney described a case in which her client was instructed to get 100 letters of support before his waiver petition would be approved. When his wife relayed the message to the attorney, the attorney told her, "No, that is not right. There is no such thing. I am not going to submit 100 identical letters." The clients fired her and went with another attorney—one who agreed to send the letters—and sure enough, a year later, the first attorney got the man's approval notice in the mail.

Families' suspicions that their cases are treated capriciously are reinforced by innumerable errors reportedly made by immigration agents. Beth and Jorge, for example, were denied a hardship waiver based on another family's evidence. Alberto's immigration parole documents were lost. Hector was told to drop off his waiver packet at the U.S. consulate in Juárez, only to be turned away with instructions to send it through the mail when he got there (an error that cost him and Cynthia $250 in airplane tickets).

The most egregious example of the system's apparent indifference to its effect on couples involves the dramatic and unanticipated lengthening of processing times from 3 weeks to up to 15 months in 2011. As Beth put it, "the wheels came off in Juárez" when U.S. adjudicators at the Juárez consulate needed to return suddenly to the United States because their own visas allowing them to be in Mexico were expiring. Their sudden departure created a backlog of waivers in need of processing and lengthened wait times from a few weeks to several months without any warning or explanation to families in the process. This unexplained delay led to prolonged separation for Anya and Enrique, Pamela and Victor, Beth and Jorge, and Grace and Carlos; all of them were caught up in this backlog, unexpectedly separated for months and unable to find out why.

The Juárez Wives

Families interpret the vagaries of consular processing as an example of extreme governmental inefficiency. And, indeed, it seems likely that U.S. immigration agents are overworked, underresourced, and themselves governed by onerous, arbitrary, and opaque policies. In 2011, the year that Victor left for processing in Juárez, more than 23,000 hardship waiver petitions were filed with DHS. Approximately two-thirds, or more than 15,000 of those petitions, were adjudicated at the U.S. consulate in Ciudad Juárez, which was staffed with only three adjudicators and one field office director (U.S. Department of Homeland Security 2012). If all three adjudicators worked 40 hours per week for 50 weeks of the year, they would each have processed an average of more than 20 waiver petitions per day, or 2½ waiver petitions every hour.

Still, if bureaucratic indifference "is the rejection of common humanity" (Herzfeld 1992, 1), inefficiency in the way that families' cases are handled can be interpreted as a communication to family members that they do not deserve to be treated with care and respect. According to this interpretation, inefficiency and indifference are not failures of the system so much as a logical extension of the dehumanization of undocumented immigrants and, by association, their lawfully resident family members. As a result, consular processing both upholds the value of U.S. citizenship through the criterion of extreme hardship and degrades U.S. citizens in the process.

Indeed, it is often only when they submit to immigration programs that U.S. citizens learn that they have no right to family under immigration laws at all. This realization can be profoundly unsettling and even politically alienating. "I have had a ton of times that I've felt betrayal from the U.S.," one woman, Danielle, explained, "I have thought to myself, 'I'm an American citizen and my government is keeping me away from the man I love and the father of my child. Why?'" Beth said that she "feel[s] this huge sense of guilt as a U.S. citizen. This is my country and my country's laws that are putting these people in this situation." While Isaiah awaited the waiver decision in Mexico, Jane stayed with her parents, who tried to distract her by taking her to performances near their Missouri vacation home. "But the shows," Jane said, "start off with something like 'God Bless America.' [And she told her parents] 'I think I'll puke if I have to sit through that.'" One U.S. citizen became so angered by her experiences with the immigration system that she no longer votes, shunning what is perhaps the most emblematic practice of democratic citizenship. Indeed, it is telling that a process of political incorporation can be so onerous that it actually estranges U.S. citizens from feelings of national belonging and participation (Gomberg-Muñoz 2016).

Whiteness and middle-class status offer little insulation from routine bureaucratic humiliation. Natalie, for example, describes her family as "upper middle class," and she has had few encounters with state authorities. "I've never gotten anything more than a traffic ticket," she explained, "So, like, this is very new to be on that side, talking to a federal agent, you know. That's not something that I've had any experience with at all." Now in her forties, Natalie finds herself separated from her husband by a five-year unwaivable bar on his reentry, and she has learned that her citizenship, race, class privilege, and ample social capital do nothing to safeguard his return. "I grew up in relative luxury in the U.S., and I have never been hungry a day in my life," she said, "These past three years [without my husband] have been the hardest period of my life. . . . I'm a U.S. citizen, . . . but my government has been incredibly difficult in every way, shape, or form with this entire experience."

In wider society, U.S. citizens find that their situation is, at best, poorly understood and, at worst, considered by some a fitting punishment for their decision to marry an undocumented immigrant.[1] Anya said that one of the hardest things about being separated from Enrique was "the fact that nobody could understand why I was so upset, and, 'What's my problem anyways? Six months is nothing; people are separated for years.' . . . It was hard for me to find support other than [the Juárez Wives Club]." When Cynthia and Hector's case took over their lives for the better part of two years, forcing Cynthia to take a leave of absence from medical school, she said, "I think a lot of my family members and his family members were sympathizing with him and his situation in Mexico, but I really didn't feel like there was any support for me. [No one said] 'I know it's hard on you, too.' They just thought, you're fine, you're in Chicago, you're still in school, you're okay. . . . [But] both of our lives were at stake, even though people don't realize that." Alienated from their social support systems by this process, in 2011 U.S.-citizen spouses turned to each other.

Left in the dark, separated from their spouses, and unable to access official channels, in 2011, Anya, Jane, Pamela, Beth, and more than a dozen others began communicating via an online immigration forum. There, they discovered that none of the families undertaking waiver adjudication through the Juárez consulate had received a decision in months, and operators at the National Visa Center (NVC) were giving out rote misinformation. The women branched off to form a support group, the Juárez Wives Club, for families undertaking consular processing and waiver adjudication through the Juárez consulate.

The Juárez Wives Club served a dual purpose. First, it transformed members from couples stumbling through bureaucratic hoops largely in isolation to participants in a collective seeking to empower themselves and each other through information sharing. The Wives began keeping track of everything related to their cases: notices from the NVC and DHS and the dates and cities in which the letters were postmarked, phone numbers for the NVC and DHS, advice from attorneys, sample hardship letters, reasons for denials and referrals, names of congresspeople who would help with cases, and even lists of legislators who were withholding support of comprehensive immigration reform. The Wives created a "moral economy of exchange" (Bourgois and Schonberg 2009; Horton 2015), in which information and documents were circulated on the site to help families penetrate the bureaucracy of immigration procedures. Through these practices of exchange, several of the founding members became lay experts in immigration law; one woman even went on to become a licensed immigration attorney following her experience working on her husband's consular processing case. Together, the Wives built a body of collective knowledge that challenged the sequestration of information by U.S. immigration authorities and even surpassed that of their own attorneys.

Second, the Juárez Wives Club provided a space for families undertaking immigration processing to commiserate and validate each other's experiences. "Immigration sucks. I am just missing my [loved one] today," reads one post on the site. Several Wives contributed sympathetic responses below. Another, dated December 25, 2012, offered comfort: "Merry Christmas JW's. For those of you separated this Christmas, it gets better. Last year we were separated by this process and this Christmas we are together again." In addition to tips for putting together waiver petitions, the documents on the site also share more intimate information, such as favorite recipes and a list of the names and birthdates of babies born to Juárez Wives while their spouses were away. One document, entitled "What song reminds you of that loved one?" contains a list of love songs in both English and Spanish, some supplemented with a brief explanation: "(hubby dedicated this one to me)". Separated from their spouses and often isolated from family and friends, the Wives cultivated much-needed support and consolation with each other on the site.

Model Citizens, Model Families

Through their participation in the Juárez Wives Club, U.S. citizen women also learned to leverage their citizenship status, as well as their roles as wives and mothers, to garner political support for their cases. Many U.S. citizens like Anya and Natalie appealed to sympathetic congresspeople to intervene on their behalf, usually with limited success. Others have taken to the media and blogosphere, where U.S. citizens who are separated from their undocumented spouses or "exiled" abroad, like Jane, have received regional and national coverage in newspaper and radio stories.

As they enter into national debates on immigration reform, U.S. citizens tap into potent symbolism surrounding the "immigrant family," which is central to mainstream immigrant rights campaigns

(Pallares 2014). Immigrant family discourse evokes heteronormative and middle-class "family values" to contest deportation and family separation, frequently silencing undocumented people while casting U.S.-citizen family members, often children, as family spokespeople (Pallares 2014). These mobilizations uphold an ideal "citizen family," undergirded by long-standing gendered, class, racial, sexual, and biodeterministic norms (Yanagisako and Collier 1987; Pallares 2014; Salcido and Menjívar 2012; Stack 1974; Weston 1997).

In mobilizations for mixed-status couples, the immigrant family is discursively recast as the "American family," utilizing U.S. nationalism to boost political support. U.S. citizens in these campaigns strategically deploy their national identities as Americans and U.S. citizens, as well as their gendered roles as wives and mothers, to heighten sympathy for their cases. In 2013, I helped gather stories for an unsuccessful campaign to provide select families with relief from the bars on reentry, and I asked some of my study participants to contribute. Heather opened her story by writing, "As a US citizen I vote, as a hard-working American I pay taxes, as a wife I love unconditionally, and as

FIGURE 5.2 Children ask for their father's release outside of a Florida detention center. Photograph by Steve Pavey, Hope in Focus Photography. www.stevepavey.com/.

a mother I nurture my child." In this mash-up of hegemonic values, Heather not only invoked her formal citizenship status, but also made claims to "economic citizenship" as a hard worker and taxpayer, as well as value-laden claims to family as a loving wife and nurturing mother.

U.S. citizens also use their status as wives and mothers to challenge the authority of lawmakers who, they say, are ill informed about the toll that immigration processing takes on families. "[Congresspeople] don't live it," Natalie stated. "It's like asking men what's best for women's health care, or asking white people what's best for African Americans. They don't live it. We live it. Only we can speak to this issue with authority because we're the ones who live it." As she contributes to a national organization that advocates for mixed-status families, Natalie evokes her lived experience in a mixed-status family to legitimize her authority on the destructive effects of U.S. immigration processing.

Like many women, Natalie also experienced the exclusion of her spouse as an affront to her own status as a U.S. citizen. Rejecting the idea that she should have to write syrupy sweet tales of love and dependence, Natalie said, "For me what's most important about this is that I'm a U.S. citizen, and I should have rights and due process with my spouse." Another U.S. citizen, Wendy, declared, "Officially, this is my application, not my husband's. . . . So for me, I feel like—well, it's not a feeling. It's very practical. These are *my rights* being trampled on." In these statements, Natalie and Wendy point up the contradiction inherent to policies that claim to value family unity for U.S. citizens yet deny U.S. citizens like them the ability to be with their spouses. Still, although it is politically expedient, the assertion that U.S. citizens deserve their families *because they are U.S. citizens* has important implications.

When U.S. citizens strategically identify themselves as citizen wives and mothers, they uphold distinctions between statuses and reinforce the idea that citizenship is a legitimate basis on which to distribute rights. In this way, wittingly or not, U.S. citizens like Heather, Wendy, and Natalie legitimize the very policies that have excluded their undocumented spouses in the first place. Others, such as Beth, reject the idea that family unity should be a privilege of citizenship. "One of the things that drives me absolutely nuts is when people are like, 'You deserve to be approved,'" Beth said. "It's like, well, everyone deserves to be approved. Everyone deserves to be with their family."

Changes to the System

As a result of prolonged campaigns by mixed-status families, including several Juárez Wives, significant changes were recently made to the hardship waiver program. In 2010, USCIS began instituting a centralized filing system, called the "Lockbox," which is meant to streamline intake and initial processing of immigration forms and fees. Rather than having to travel to Juárez, for example, to submit certain forms in person, many forms can now be sent through the mail in the United States. If it meets its goals, the Lockbox system will make it easier for families to submit some forms, and it will expedite the initial screening of immigration applications and waiver petitions.

The second major change to consular processing with a hardship waiver involves a shift in the order of the steps. As of March 2013, instead of leaving the United States, attending a consular interview, and then submitting a hardship waiver application abroad, qualifying applicants can do the waiver processing first from within the United States. If they are approved, they then leave the United States for their consular interview already knowing that their bar has been waived. This change, called the provisional waiver program, was made in response to pressure from families like those described above and is designed to reduce the length and uncertainty of family separation. This change was instituted after most of my fieldwork was completed; however, I know two families, including Stephanie and Javier, who have undertaken this program with great success and were separated for less than a week.

However, early data have also found a high rate of denial: nearly 40 percent of initial applications to the provisional waiver program have been denied (Schreiber and Wheeler 2013). Of the denied applicants, almost half have been denied for "reason to believe" that they meet grounds of inadmissibility other than the 10-year bar for unlawful presence. This suspicion appears to be largely triggered by a record of arrests and/or convictions that would not ordinarily meet a ground of inadmissibility, such as repeat traffic violations (Schreiber and Wheeler 2013), and USCIS has said that it is working to resolve this issue with additional trainings for adjudicators. About 40 percent of families who are denied are deemed to have failed to establish extreme hardship (Schreiber and Wheeler 2013). Families that are denied in the provisional waiver program may still undertake the old procedure, in which the applicant leaves first and then waits outside the United States while the case is processed.

Conclusion

For families whose hardship waiver petition is approved, the pathway to lawful status is nearly complete. On approval, the consulate runs one final background check with DHS, which will delay some applicants, especially from countries that the United States associates with "terrorism," such as Pakistan or Iran, for several more months. And even approved applicants can always be turned away at a U.S. port of entry, although I have never encountered such a case.

The lives of families who undertake consular processing will never be the same. Those whose waiver petitions are denied, like Beth and Jorge and Jane and Isaiah, must make tough decisions about whether to continue trying, live apart, or relocate so that they can be together. Families that are approved get to reunite lawfully, but often must work to rebuild their relationships after a long and difficult separation. Moreover, they have a new set of hurdles to face: learning to be legal. I turn to this stage in the next chapter.

CHAPTER 6

Life After Legal Status

René and Molly

In 2014, as ever, René and Molly's 4th of July party was a big success. Surrounded by family and friends, they celebrated the 238th anniversary of U.S. independence. It was also the 19th summer that René lived in Chicago, the 12th anniversary of his marriage to Molly, and the 6th year that had passed since they initiated immigration processing. René remains undocumented.

René and Molly continue to hold out hope that one day they will be able to legalize his status. René dreams of seeing his parents in Mexico and taking his children to meet them. He would also like to get a better job, one with paid vacations and a retirement account, maybe as an industrial engineer. "I don't ask for money, I don't ask for anything, I just want [my friends and me] to be legal so we can get better jobs, and go outside, and drive." René's wish to drive legally, at least, was granted in 2014, after passage of a state bill that allows undocumented Illinois drivers to obtain licenses. René's Illinois license is but one more indication of his belonging in Chicago, alongside his family, friends, home, and long-time job here.

Yet every year that immigration reform legislation fails to pass, René's hopes of becoming legal without leaving his family dim. "I think that eventually I will go to Juárez," he told me during our final interview. "What if you can't come back for ten years?" I asked. "Either way, I would come back," he replied with a shrug.

Enrique and Anya

Anya and Enrique spent four months waiting for a decision on their hardship waiver petition. Then, one December afternoon as Anya was heading to her second job, she saw a DHL truck turn onto her block; she turned around and raced back home. A letter from USCIS was waiting for her in the mailbox. "So I grab this letter, and soon as I see it, I start bawling," she recalled. "And finally I locate the huge thing that says, 'Approval Notice' and locate it where it says, 'You have been approved based on these grounds and your waiver has been approved based on these grounds.' And I'm bawling and shaking, and tears are streaming down my face." Enrique stayed in Mexico for another two months before his visa was finally issued. Then, in February 2012, he came home to Anya.

Enrique and Anya have spent the ensuing years deciding how to move forward with their lives. They want to have children someday, but are holding off until their careers are established. In the meantime, Anya has decided to apply to law school—a long-time ambition of hers that she feels able to pursue now that Enrique's future in the United States is secured. Enrique has also been pursuing new career goals. When he returned to Chicago, he went back to his job at the restaurant, but he also began taking evening classes to become a certified personal trainer and dietician. On the weekends, Enrique has been running in marathons. For Enrique and Anya, getting legal status has opened a world of possibilities. "The fact that we went on vacation, the fact that he has his driver's license, the fact that he's able to go to school, those are all things that have definitely changed our lives," Anya explained.

Yet, Anya added, "Everything changed, and nothing changed" with Enrique's legal status. Anya believes that, sometimes, couples look to legalization as a magic wand that will fix their problems. But "happiness is an inside job," she said. "Whoever you were before you got papers, that's who you are with papers, too." Some couples struggle with this realization, she says, and she and Enrique have, too. "Ultimately," she concludes, "we have a strong enough marriage that it survived."

Cynthia and Hector

After their rocky start with immigration processing, Hector spent a year and a half in Mexico while their case was processed. During that time, he and

Cynthia struggled to keep their marriage together through the emotional and financial strain of indefinite separation. When their waiver petition was finally approved in the spring of 2013, Cynthia planned him a welcome-home party, "I made a huge pot of pozole from scratch," she remembered. "Once I got the approval," she said, "it just felt like, okay, my life can go back to normal. Now I can go on to do whatever I want. And he'll be back, and we'll have a family, and we'll be set. At least, that's what you think."

Although Hector was relieved to be home, it took him several months to readjust to his life in Chicago. He was anxious to return to work at the diner right away, but he had to wait two months for his social security card to arrive. When he did go back to work, he was promoted to a managerial position, with a raise and health insurance to boot. At home, he and Cynthia worked on getting comfortable with each other again. "I remember he would say, you know, 'I am happy,'" Cynthia said, "but there was strangeness. Like he still—he realized that things had changed." Hector had been home for a year when Cynthia and I talked for the final time, and they were still healing from the process. "Once they come back, it doesn't mean that everything goes back to normal," Cynthia said. "You have to make your own normal again."

Marco and Tanya

After 18 months of waiting in Mexico, Marco's waiver petition was approved. He returned to Juárez once more to pick up his passport, now stamped with a U.S. visa, and he called Tanya as soon as he held it in his hand. "She was so happy, she cried," Marco recalled. "My daughter was happy, too. She said, 'Daddy, I really miss you, and I want you here to cook my pierogis.'" As Marco went through the border checkpoint with his new visa, the agent told him, "Welcome to the United States. You can enter by land, air, and sea." "Thank you," Marco replied, and he passed into the United States legally for the first time.

But Marco soon learned that his troubles were not over. He had not been granted a regular immigrant visa, but a conditional one, good for only two years. In the meantime, he was on probation, and his behavior was being closely monitored. To complicate matters, Marco's new visa only has his first surname printed on it, and thus the names on Marco's passport and visa did not match—a common problem for Latin Americans who use two surnames. As a result, when Marco travels, he is routinely pulled into U.S. immigration offices and questioned. "It's like they think I'm a terrorist," he said. In addition, the Illinois Department of Motor Vehicles accused Marco of fraud because his old Illinois license also had two surnames instead of one, and his new driver license was canceled just two weeks after it was issued. As a result, Marco lost his new job as a commercial truck driver.

Without a driver license, without a job, on immigration probation, and accused of fraud, a familiar fear crept over Marco again. "It was better when I didn't have papers," Marco said. "I feel like a criminal." He and Tanya hired another attorney to fight the fraud charge; eventually Marco was cleared of fraud, and the cancelation of his license was reduced to a one-year suspension. Still, the shadow of suspicion clings to Marco. His newfound ability to travel back and forth is inhibited by intense questioning every time he reenters the United States; the fraud charge, although cleared, has pushed his auto insurance costs through the roof; and the Internal Revenue Service, unconvinced that Marco Luís Kalecki Orozco and Marco Luís Kalecki are the same person, has placed a lien on their house for nonpayment of taxes. "This is not what I had in mind," Marco told me during our final interview; "This is not over yet."

Pamela and Victor

Victor stepped off the plane in Chicago just hours after leaving Juárez, and he saw his wife and children for the first time in nearly six months. It was a surreal experience. "I saw you," he told Pamela, "but I didn't see you. I could not even figure out where I was." When he was in Mexico, he and Pamela had planned for their reunion; for the kids, they decided, they would try to make things as normal as possible. But "to be gone out of someone's life for six months," Pamela said, "you might think, well, that's just a drop in a big bucket of water, but it made a difference." Their relationship had changed. They found it difficult to get along at first, Pamela said, and "we had to sit down and say, 'Either we need to come to an agreement, or we're going to have to get some help,' because it was such a hard adjustment period."

Two years later, Pamela said that her marriage to Victor is stronger than ever. After making it through immigration processing, they no longer fight about petty issues. Also, they learned how to survive on one income while Victor was gone and have been saving more money since his return. But above all, Pamela said, the process has "made me realize what I have and how precious that time is." For Pamela and Victor, the separation, the cost, and the anxiety were ultimately worth it. Pamela said that Victor's legal status "means that nobody can take my husband away. It doesn't mean everything, but it means that nobody can take us apart. It means that he can breathe. It means he can go to work and come home, and he's not looking behind him. It means that when I say the prayer in the morning that I hope my husband comes home safe, I am like any other wife saying it."

In the end, the pursuit of lawful status is, as Pamela put it, simply a quest to be like "anyone else"—to live without the specter of deportation lurking over your shoulder. When processing is successful, lawful status not only reduces the risk of family separation, but also can open possibilities for safe travel and upward socioeconomic mobility. It enhances a family's long-term security, making it easier to plan for the future. But, as Pamela also noted, legal status does not mean everything. Being like anyone else in the United States means navigating a socioeconomic landscape beset by inequality, limited opportunity, and concentrated segregation and violence. On a more mundane level, it also usually means living on a budget, arguing with your partner, and worrying about your children. As Anya observed, lawful status is no magic fix for these ordinary trials. In this final ethnographic chapter, I explore how families experience both the promises and the limitations of newly lawful status. I also revisit families whose processing cases were denied or indefinitely placed on hold, and I explore how these couples manage their lives apart or abroad.

The Greatest Feeling Ever

People whom I interviewed variously described undocumented status as "a weight on your shoulders," "a veil over your eyes," and "having your legs tied with a cord." For many, attaining legal status lifts the weight, draws back the veil, and unties the cord "so now you can run." It can be profoundly liberating. Abril said that getting a green card was "the greatest feeling ever. . . . Nothing stops me now. I can travel. I can work. I can do whatever I want."

For members of mixed-status families, the conferral of lawful status means that the family can stay together in the place they call home. Anya and Enrique, Cynthia and Hector, Marco and Tanya and their children, and Pamela and Victor and their children can go forward with their lives with little fear of family separation. It is hard to overestimate the relief for families long accustomed to living in a state of uncertainty. Cynthia, for example, no longer suffers from "constant anxiety about what's going to happen to me or what's going to happen to my family." This relief is experienced not only in the abstract, but also concretely as people undertake everyday, mundane tasks, such as buying beer at a baseball game, passing through security checkpoints in corporate buildings, and, above all, driving legally (Jose Angel N. 2014). "That's the first thing I thought about, 'I'm going to be able to drive with a license without being afraid!'" explained Enrique. Likewise, U.S.-citizen spouses are no longer plagued with worry when their partners drive to work or leave to run errands. Grace explained that, for her, Carlos's legal status means "I'm not worried about him being arrested anymore. I think the thing for me was always thinking, what if he gets caught driving again? I might have to go get him, bail him out, what's going to happen to him? . . . Now it's like, I don't even think about it anymore. It's, like, it's a relief. It's almost like now I know I can have a stable household. . . . I'm not afraid."

Attaining legal status also allows people to reconnect with loved ones they left behind in their countries of origin. For people who have been trapped in the United States and unable to visit family members back home for years and decades, being able to travel is one of the most meaningful benefits of legalization. As one woman, Lucy, explained, "This country [the United States] is gigantic. It's gigantic, but it's still a cage for those of us who can't leave. . . . It might be a big cage, but it's a cage all the same." When Lucy got the phone call notifying her that her 10-year wait for a visa was over, time stood still while the news sunk in. "When that moment arrived, my god, it was—No. No, it was incredible." That night, Lucy and her husband began planning a trip to their native Colombia to visit family members they had been missing for more than a decade.

The ability to travel was also profoundly important to Veronica. With her family in Mexico, the pain of Veronica's failing marriage was compounded by her isolation. Veronica leaned on her mom for moral support, calling her on the phone daily and often talking with her late into the night. She was not allowed to travel abroad for three years while her case was pending, and she desperately missed being with her mom in person. The first thing that Veronica did when she got her green card was to book a ticket to spend two weeks with her mother in Mexico. Veronica's lawful status also meant a release from her dependency on Francisco, and she began the process of putting bills in her own name and transferring her apartment lease and car note from Francisco's name to hers. With these small steps toward independence, Veronica has begun the process of healing and reclaiming her life. "Having residency makes me feel free," she said, "When my documents came, I felt like I could go outside and say, 'Here I am, and I exist.' Even when I go to the airport now [she mimics walking upright and proudly], 'I'm a resident!' Seriously, it changes things. It changes things."

With lawful status, the "cages" that enclose people open, allowing them to travel not only to reconnect with family, but also for more lighthearted reasons. When Marco returned to his family after a year and a half in Mexico, he was concerned about the toll that processing had taken on Tanya. He said, "I looked at my wife, [who was] all stressed out from everything that had happened, from working two jobs," and he told her, "Let's go to Cancún. I have papers now, let's go to Cancún." And Marco took his family on a much-needed weeklong vacation before coming home to find himself accused of fraud and subject to ongoing legal entanglements with immigration authorities.

Lawful status facilitates mobility not only across distance, but also forward in time because families long suspended in a state of uncertainty can plan for the future. Enrique says, "You see more options ahead of you. . . . You see more doors open." When Cynthia received word that Hector's waiver had been approved, she wept with relief. "I thought, oh my god, after so long, after all of this, I'm going to be able to stay in Chicago, in the U.S., and he's going to be able to come back. . . . Now I can, you know, now I can be a [medical school student] again." But planning for the future involves getting readjusted to life together and making difficult decisions about careers, homes, and family planning.

Readjusting in the Aftermath of Legalization

The first few months after processing are an adjustment period, during which time mixed-status families members must learn to live together again. Months and years apart can create a breeding ground for misunderstanding and resentment; all of the love and relief at being lawfully reunited does not erase the pain and trauma of prolonged separation.

Cynthia said that when Hector returned, she "had a lot of resentment, I remember. So the next few months, I think we were just trying to fix our relationship and get close to each other again." She continued, "I think we play into this fantasy that once you get your papers your life is fixed. And it's not. Like yes, you no longer have to walk with fear or drive with fear that someone is going to deport you or separate you from your family. But all your other issues are still there. And I couldn't tell people, because I just felt like my fairytale story couldn't be disrupted by the reality of complicated relationships." Anya and Enrique also worked hard on their marriage after processing. Anya explained, "I don't want to sound cheesy, but there's him and me, and then there's also our marriage as a whole, like there's a soul; our marriage has a soul, and I felt like that was being torn apart completely during the immigration process."

The persistence of marital issues in the aftermath of processing is enough to strain even the strongest of relationships. Most of the couples that I interviewed struggled successfully to make it through this period, but Wendy and Paolo have separated. Guillermo and Marie remain together but worry that their relationship has suffered irreparable damage. "Was it worth it?" I asked them as we discussed the aftermath of Guillermo's processing experience. "No," said Marie quickly. "Probably not," agreed Guillermo, looking at his wife. This period is so challenging that some members of the Juárez Wives Club branched off to form a support group, Life after Legalization, to help couples survive the trials of readjustment following immigration processing.

Marital relations are not the only ones that can become strained by legalization. When one member of the family becomes legal, his or her siblings, cousins, parents, and friends often remain undocumented. In other words, legalization also creates mixed-status families from formerly all-undocumented ones, a situation that can produce feelings of guilt and bitterness. Many people refrain from discussing their lawful status openly in front of undocumented family members and friends for fear of seeming boastful or creating resentment. Others describe feeling a sort of "survivor's guilt" about becoming legal when so many of their friends and family members cannot—a feeling that is exacerbated by the arbitrary-seeming nature of legalization criteria.

For example, after more than a decade of being undocumented, Lourdes's fortune changed without warning. In 2012, a group of teenagers assaulted her younger brother, and as a result, Lourdes and her family became eligible to get a U visa. A U visa is a category of conditional visa that undocumented people can apply for if they are victims of a crime and provide testimony in court that can aid in a criminal conviction. The U visa is good for four years, and at the end of that period, Lourdes and her family will be eligible to apply for lawful permanent residency. "[One phone] call later," she said, "I'm on the other side."

Lourdes felt conflicted. One the one hand, she shared in her mother and brother's joy at being able to work legally and travel safely. On the other hand, she was conscious that the circumstances of her legalization were beyond her control and that her friends were unable to share in her good fortune. When her U visa arrived, Lourdes kept the news to herself for several days before posting it on Facebook. Then, she explained, "my Facebook status got more than 100 likes. And I felt kind of angry at the people who commented or who would send me messages like, 'Congratulations!' Because it was just like, no, you don't get it. I didn't do anything. I just have this thing now. I didn't get it because of my own work or merit, I got it because my brother was the victim of a crime." For Lourdes, any gratification at becoming legal was tempered by the persistent vulnerability of so many friends and loved ones who were equally deserving of relief but shut out of avenues to lawful status.

With the hurdle of immigration processing out of the way, newly legal people and their family members must decide what to do next. Most people want to resume working as soon as they can, but where? With debt and bills from immigration processing mounting, newly legal workers must decide whether to return to their old jobs or test the trope that legal status opens pathways to upward socioeconomic mobility.

Movin' on Up?

It is widely accepted in both immigrant communities and labor migration scholarship that a lack of legal status constrains work opportunities and funnels undocumented people into low-paying and insecure jobs (Basch et al. 1994; De Genova 2005; Gomberg-Muñoz 2011; Heyman 1998, 2001; Massey et al. 2002; Portes and Walton 1981; Sassen-Koob 1981; Zlolniski 2003). The logical extension of this argument is that when undocumented people become legal, those constraints on upward mobility will ease, if not lift altogether. Indeed, my study participants nearly universally agreed that one of the benefits of becoming legal is greater access to more desirable jobs.

There is some quantitative evidence to support the idea that legalization of formerly undocumented workers results in more job flexibility and gains in income (Chavez 2008; Powers et al. 1998). Yet the degree to which such gains are attributable to legal status alone is not clear: they are probably at least partially explained by workers' cumulative time on the job (see also Hagan 1994). In addition, such advances are usually modest and many legalized immigrants continue to face serious limitations on their opportunities, often remaining in the same low-wage jobs that they held as undocumented workers (Kytina 2002). And, of course, factors other than legal status—such as race, gender, education, and English-language proficiency—continue to be significant predictors of occupation and income level among immigrants in the United States (Mehta et al. 2002; Powers et al. 1998). My data broadly support these findings.

I interviewed 25 people who had work experience when they were undocumented and then as lawful residents or DACA recipients; 18 of them experienced upward mobility after they gained work eligibility—typically quite modest. Five continued to work in the same jobs for roughly the same pay, and the remaining 2 experienced downward mobility. A closer look at the stories behind these figures offers some insight into the variation of job market experiences of newly legal immigrants and suggests some reasons for the variation.

For many of my study participants, lawful status provided access to jobs that had been previously off limits. On returning from Juárez, both Hector and Enrique were promoted to managerial positions at the restaurants where they had long worked. Interestingly, their mobility was not a result of changing employers or companies, but of their employers' association of undocumented workers with some positions and not others in the company. Once the men attained legal status, they were moved from menial positions to more supervisory ones, although their education, skills, and levels of experience had not changed. Veronica was also offered a promotion at the community organization where she had worked for years, although in her case, the promotion was a result of her newfound ability to travel freely and, thus, to manage an important binational project.

Other experiences of upward mobility occur when workers gain access to companies that typically exclude undocumented workers during the hiring process. For example, Ben was able to get a job as a maintenance worker with the University of Illinois system once he got legal status, and Rosita got a job at a hospital after becoming licensed as a Certified Nurse Assistant. Abril began working in the offices of a state senator. Guillermo moved from restaurant work to a job with a package delivery company that screens all applicants through E-Verify, an online work eligibility verification program. Guillermo now earns three times his old income and has health insurance and a retirement plan to boot.

Yet, Guillermo points out, his ability to get the new job was not a result of his lawful status alone; his father-in-law is a supervisor at the company, and he "put in a good word" for Guillermo. Guillermo's father-in-law could not have advocated for Guillermo's hire before without jeopardizing his own standing in the company, but once Guillermo was legal, he could use his social capital to help his daughter's family. When it comes to getting a job in the United States, "It's who you know," observed Guillermo's wife, Marie. Indeed, social capital, and particularly the help of well-established in-laws like Guillermo's, was instrumental in the upward mobility of many of my study participants. One young man got a job in the union trades through his well-connected father-in-law. Luis and his friend Sam both got jobs through their social contacts after they were granted work permits. Sam explained, "I think when I ended up getting a work permit . . ., I realized that having a work permit didn't really give me this open access to all these amazing jobs." Instead, he said, "You get the jobs that you're exposed to by your circles, and they can put in a good word for you . . . so for a lot of [undocumented] people they just went from working in [a] service sector job without a social security number to having [a social security number] and staying in the same jobs." These stories suggest that the benefits of legal status are not evenly distributed, but are greater for immigrants who can bolster their job applications with personal recommendations from well-connected friends and family members.

In fact, upward mobility was most consistent and substantial for my study participants who had both ample U.S. social capital and high levels of education. Leticia, for example, came to the United States as a teenager, graduated from a Chicago high school, and then went on to finish college. Although she had a bachelor's degree, Leticia worked in retail until she was able to legalize her status; then she got a job doing community outreach for a Chicago-area university. After Luis got DACA, he was able to parlay his college education into a position with the Chicago Public School System; he came highly recommended for that position through his contacts at the university and Chicago-area community organizations. Both Leticia and Luis had plentiful U.S. cultural capital, such as English fluency and literacy, as well as U.S. social capital, including abundant contacts in and around Chicago who could connect them with jobs.

I also interviewed people who were professionals in their country of origin but experienced downward mobility when they migrated to the United States and then resumed professional life after legalization. For example, Lucy was a well-paid project manager for a large company in her native Colombia. When she came to the United States, Lucy worked cleaning airport bathrooms until she became so fearful of immigration authorities that she quit her job. She then volunteered in her children's school but did not pursue paid employment. When Lucy and her husband attained lawful status, Lucy promptly started her own business. So did Sal, who had been a teacher in El Salvador but worked in restaurants when he came to the United States. After Sal was able to legalize his status under 1986's IRCA, he opened his own insurance agency and, as a result, he says proudly, was able to put his two sons through college.

As legalization opens new possibilities, people may also find it easier or more rewarding to pursue education or training in hopes of upward mobility in the future. Three of my participants got their GED after they legalized their status, and many more began or continued to take English-language courses. For Enrique, it was learning English that provided the earliest and most tangible benefits in the job market, allowing him to move from factory work to his job at the restaurant. He explains, "When I started to go to school, I started to get it more. . . . And, yeah, when I felt more comfortable speaking English, I got a job as a restaurant busboy and, you know, that's a lot more money than what you make in a factory." Newly legal and now fluent in English, Enrique hopes to expand his horizons even further as he takes courses to become licensed as a dietician and personal trainer.

Some undocumented workers who were content with their jobs resume them after legalization. Indeed, I interviewed two workers who said that job mobility was an important benefit to legalization, yet remained in the same jobs they had when they were undocumented. Still others remain in the same industry but earn higher incomes because they now refuse to tolerate overtly exploitative working conditions.

Carlos, for example, worked installing and cleaning ducts when he was undocumented; his pay was low and his employer often failed to pay him overtime wages. After Carlos legalized his status, he went back to duct work but for a different company. Now, Carlos is not afraid to tell his employer, "Hey, you know what, my check is short two hours. You guys forgot to pay me for this overtime that I worked." Carlos's story supports the claim, which is often invoked by immigrant rights advocates, that legal status can help protect immigrant workers from workplace abuses.

Conversely, the ability to insist that employers abide by labor laws may hurt the job prospects of some newly legal workers. María, for example, was one of two workers whom I interviewed who experienced downward mobility after legalization. When María was undocumented, she worked for an agency that farms out workers to factories on a temporary basis. By all accounts, temporary factory work is one of the most degrading and poorly paying jobs available to workers in Chicago, and María and her family lived in poverty for many years before María was able to legalize her status through a U visa. María's dream, when her work permit arrived, was to open a photography studio. But she quickly learned that with no wealth and no credit history, banks were unwilling to lend her the money she would need to buy a camera and other equipment. Discouraged, María returned to the temp agencies, but was surprised to learn that they were no longer interested in hiring her. "What's happening now," she explained, "is that the companies don't want people who they have to give medical [insurance] or [unemployment] benefits to. It's easier for them, because there are so many people who are going to work without benefits." María has little formal education, is not proficient in English, and does not have well-connected family members or friends in Chicago. For her, legalization is no ticket out of poverty. Indeed, María's job prospects may actually be more limited than before, since some employers at the bottom of the job market prefer an undocumented labor force to a legal one (Gomberg-Muñoz and Nussbaum-Barberena 2011; Ticktin 2006). In fact, when I recounted María's story to Juan, an organizer who works with low-paid undocumented workers in Chicago, he nodded knowingly. "Oh, yes," he said, "[getting a job] is more difficult when you have papers."

The other person who experienced downward mobility as a result of legalization is Marco. After Marco's driver's license was suspended because his green card only had one of his surnames on it, he lost his new job as a truck driver. In addition, Marco and his wife had to pay lawyer's fees to fight the fraud charge and higher costs for auto insurance; they are worried they will lose their house to the Internal Revenue Service. Together, these expenses further eroded their already-tenuous financial security. If Marco can clear up his record, his job woes are likely to be temporary, and he and his family may experience upward mobility over time.

Because the notion that upward mobility will result from legalization is widely accepted, failure to obtain a better-paying or higher-status job can come as a bitter disappointment. Marco was frustrated and depressed when he came home from Juárez only to lose his job and continue battling with U.S. agencies on several fronts. Another young man felt like a failure when he was unable to parlay his lawful status into a better job. He enrolled in a GED course, but quit when he found the workload to be overwhelming. He stayed in his job as a restaurant cook. Two years after immigration processing, he was caught in a rut and demoralized. As with Marco and María, the reality of lawful status has not yet lived up to its promise for this young worker, and the "American Dream" remains out of reach.

There is a final way in which legal status affected the socioeconomic stability of my study participants: some newly legal parents felt more able to apply for public benefits for their U.S.-citizen children. The ability to apply for benefits does not technically change with legalization: U.S.-citizen children are eligible for benefits regardless of their parents' status, whereas lawful permanent resident adults typically remain ineligible for public benefits for at least five years. Still, research has shown that many undocumented parents are fearful of applying for benefits because they believe (with good reason) that receiving government assistance could hurt any future chance they might have for legalization (Dreby 2015; Fix and Zimmerman 2001; Horton 2014). With that fear lifted, parents of U.S. citizens may be more likely to take advantage of the services for which their children are eligible. Rosita said that for her, one of the most important benefits of being legal is "You can find help for the kids. You find help for food, for housing, low income housing. It's helped me with the medical card." Still, for Rosita, "Above all, number one is to find a job and make sure your kids are well." For Rosita and other low-income mothers, public benefits provide an important supplement to meager wages that legal status alone does little to boost.

Together, my study participants' experiences indicate that legalization can open pathways to modest upward socioeconomic mobility that are largely denied to undocumented people. Yet, my research also suggests that full access to these pathways is not guaranteed by lawful status alone. Instead, U.S. social and cultural capital—in particular, well-connected in-laws and English-language fluency and literacy—continue to shape the financial prospects of newly legal immigrants.

They Can Take It Away

> *"Be careful, man."*
> *"Yeah, be careful. They can take it away."*
> *"Yeah, they can take it away for any little thing, if you're driving messed up, or if you get caught with something. You have to be careful."*

This was the advice two undocumented friends gave to Stephanie's husband, Javier, when he returned home to Chicago after consular processing in Juárez. They talked about how Javier's life would change now: "You can go to Mexico, man. And now you can get a good job," and they cautioned him not to take his newfound legal status for granted, because "They can take it away." Javier's friends were not being overly cautious: of the approximately 400,000 people who have been deported each year since 2008, about 10 percent, or around 40,000 deportees annually, are lawful permanent U.S. residents (Baum et al. 2010). The advice of Javier's friends reflects a growing awareness of the vulnerability of legal immigrants to criminalization and deportation.

In those first few months after processing, people who spent many years living under the radar must now learn to be legal—to protect the documents that they endured so much to attain. When Hector returned to the United States with his visa, his attorney instructed him to behave "even better" now that he was a legal permanent resident. Hector's father-in-law, himself a former legal resident, echoed this advice, "You know, now that you have your residence, you can't be drinking and driving because they'll take it away. You have to work and pay your taxes, don't get into problems, don't have bad friends, people who are doing like illegal stuff, because just by association they can take it away." He admonished, "It's more important now than it was before, because now you actually have status. You have something to protect."

Both Javier and Hector were also advised by their attorneys to apply for U.S. citizenship as soon as they become eligible.

Marco, on immigration probation, must be especially cautious. He explained, "I have to be careful which of our friends I let in my car. I can't have any friends who have a gang [association] or who are doing any of that stuff because if I'm with them it can be detrimental to my case. That's what my lawyer told me: 'If you see anything that doesn't look right, just leave.'" This counsel is reminiscent of the advice given to undocumented immigrants to stay "under the radar" and out of trouble, and it has important political implications.

To explore these implications, let us revisit the story of Lourdes, introduced in Chapter 3. As with many undocumented youth who arrive in the United States as children, Lourdes "grew into" her status as a teenager; she "learned to be illegal" as coming-of-age experiences typical for middle-class adolescents, such as getting a driver license, traveling, and applying for college funds, were denied to her (Gonzales 2011). The pressure of her status began to build throughout her teenage years and came to a head when she graduated from high school. That's when "it all began to make sense," Lourdes said, "not being able to tell people about [abuse that is] going on at home because I'm undocumented, not being able to go to school because I'm undocumented, not being able to see my [older] brother [in Mexico] or my grandparents because I'm undocumented, not knowing what's going happen to me, because I'm undocumented." Overcome by despair, Lourdes tried to take her life that summer. Thankfully, she survived, and in the subsequent years, Lourdes helped lead mobilizations of undocumented Chicago youth who organized around the slogan "Undocumented and Unafraid." Over time, Lourdes has developed into a national leader in the U.S. immigrant rights movement.

Soon after her family was granted a U visa, Lourdes was arrested at a civil disobedience action in the state of Georgia, and when she got home, the family's lawyer confronted her. She explained, "My lawyer let me know that this could bring really bad stuff to the [U visa] case, like maybe it could get denied, not just for myself, but for my mom and brother." With her family's tenuous security on the line, Lourdes was forced to reconsider her political organizing activities. "That was the first time that I was like, whoa, my actions are not just going to impact me, but now there's this application, now there's something to lose." Lourdes, who spent years being undocumented and unafraid, has become documented, and now that her family has "something to lose," she is learning to be afraid. Scholars of migration have long argued that immigrant illegality helps to guarantee a docile and exploitable undocumented labor force. What Lourdes's story suggests is that legal status itself can function as a mechanism of control and discipline, especially when it is retractable, provisional, or conditional.

Fear of losing status is also cultivated in the process itself: as undocumented people undertake immigration processing, their relationship with immigration authorities is transformed from one largely characterized by mutual avoidance to one of intimate, regular, and prolonged surveillance. Even after the tests are completed, the records are run, and the status is conferred, close surveillance by state agents can linger indefinitely, and the effects can be unsettling.

When we left off her story in Chapter 3, Veronica was still married to Francisco, who had filed a petition for her residency but was manipulative and mean. Five days before Veronica and Francisco's two-year wedding anniversary, Francisco filed for divorce. Because Veronica had entered the United States with a temporary visa, she could adjust her status without leaving the United States, but she needed to be married to a U.S. citizen for two full years to remain eligible for the visa; divorce before that time would make her suspect for "marriage fraud." By filing for divorce before they reached that benchmark, Francisco hoped to end Veronica's two years of torment with a deportation order. But Veronica is resourceful and financially stable, and she hired an attorney to fight to keep her case open. Luckily, Veronica had saved documentation of her correspondence with Francisco throughout their courtship, and with overwhelming evidence that their relationship was legitimate, Veronica was granted conditional permanent residency.

Like Marco, Veronica is now on immigration probation. And much like a parolee, Veronica must meet regularly with an immigration agent throughout the two-year probational period. Perhaps ironically, if Francisco had physically abused her, Veronica would have been entitled to additional protection under U.S. law. Emotionally abused, Veronica must repeatedly account for the failure of her marriage during these meetings and convince immigration agents that the divorce was not her decision. Veronica is also repeatedly asked to provide evidence that her marriage to Francisco was legitimate and must continually furnish photographs, email correspondence, and evidence of their joint residence. Not surprisingly, Veronica does not like to rehash this period of her life with complete strangers, and she resents the assumption that she would marry for papers.

Thus, although Veronica is relieved that she can finally travel back and forth with her visa, she also says that she thinks about returning to Mexico and giving up her residency more now than she ever did before. "I think about how much this process has cost me," she explained. "How much it has cost me emotionally, morally. I feel like, like when people go to court and [defendants feel] guilty until proven innocent. . . . They're always asking for more proof. They are always suspicious." Rather than incorporating Veronica into the national polity, legalization has left her feeling more alienated from the United States than before.

For Veronica, a fresh start is not yet possible; immigration probation keeps her tethered to a painful past. And although the attainment of a regular, unconditional visa will put an end to her probation, only eventual naturalization as a U.S. citizen will move her out of the purview of immigration surveillance and allow her to cast off the yoke of suspicion that wears her down.

Banished

No matter how difficult their journey, people like Veronica, Enrique and Anya, Cynthia and Hector, and Guillermo and Marie might be considered lucky: their petitions were approved. In the end, they were able to reunite lawfully with family members and live where they choose. Not everyone is so fortunate; indeed, about 20 percent of hardship waiver petitions are ultimately denied (Kowalski 2015). Of course, millions more, including René and Molly, never even make it that far.

When couples' bids for legalization are delayed indefinitely or denied, they face an agonizing decision: should they move together outside of the United States or split the family and live apart? This question is greatly complicated by the presence of children who are settled and adjusted to their U.S. schools and homes and who may or may not speak a language other than English. This section revisits two couples whose attempts at legalization were denied and one whose case dragged on for six years to explore how families navigate life apart or abroad.

Jane and Isaiah

Even through the blurry lens of a computer camera, it is clear that Jane is proud of her new home. "Here is the living room," she says, moving to the laptop's side so that I can see behind her. "And over here is the kitchen," she says as moves the screen to the left. This is the home that Jane and Isaiah moved into after their hardship waiver petition was denied. It is in Toluca, Mexico.

"When I got that [denial] letter, it was almost a relief," Jane explained, "Now I have an answer . . . and you can move on with your life." (It was a relief for me, too, to hear this. I had had a series of interviews with people enduring family separation, and Jane was the first person I talked with who was not miserable.) After the denial, Jane got a job with a private "American School" in Toluca and moved to Mexico the following month to be with Isaiah. The school pays for their house and for Jane's medical care.

Jane likes her work and has developed friendships with her English-speaking coworkers; she also enjoys the weather in Toluca and the proximity of parks, stores, and walkways to their home. "I went from thinking the rest of my life was going to be lived in the town I grew up in, and all these ideas of adventure that I had when I was young were gone. And now it's like I'm having adventure; I'm doing interesting things." Best of all, Jane says, she and Isaiah are getting along better than ever. With the trauma of the case behind them, "We're just happy. We see each other, we smile, we hug, we're comfortable. We can sit silently; we can talk. It's really the best that it's ever been." In fact, Jane says, "I think I'm happier here than I would be in the States."

Not so Isaiah. Isaiah was not at home while Jane and I talked. Isaiah is rarely home, because he works from 8:00 in the morning until 7:30 in the evening (de sol á sol, or sunup to sundown, as they say in Mexico) as a construction laborer. "It's backbreaking work," Jane says, for which he gets paid the equivalent of about 100 dollars per week. "To me, this is like living easy," Jane explains, "and for him it's rough, and he feels like there are many more opportunities for him in the United States." Will they try again when Isaiah's 10-year bar expires? I ask. "Maybe. Who knows?" Jane replies. At the moment, she and Isaiah are more concerned with processing Jane's application for lawful permanent residency in Mexico.

When I speak with Jane for the final time two years later, she remains happy with her life in Toluca. And she and Isaiah have good news to share: they are four months pregnant. "Oh, wow, congratulations!" I exclaim. "Yeah, life is good," Jane smiles and pats her belly, "Life is good."

Paolo and Wendy

When Paolo and Wendy, a couple in their forties, learned that Paolo would be hit with an unwaivable five-year bar if they attempted immigration processing, they began making other plans. Their "Plan A" was to wait indefinitely and hope for immigration reform that would make it possible for Paolo to change his status. Their "Plan B" was to relocate to Brazil. To prepare, Paolo and Wendy bought a plot of land in northern Brazil, near Paolo's family, so they would have somewhere to go if they needed it. They also went through the process of getting Wendy a visa to live in Brazil and power of attorney in the United States so that she could make legal decisions on Paolo's behalf. They researched their rights and practiced what they would do if ICE agents ever showed up at their door.

Then, one morning, ICE agents did show up. Wendy held them off while Paolo hid in their bedroom. She denied the agents entry and called an attorney, who advised Paolo to request voluntary departure. With ICE agents surrounding their apartment, Wendy went outside to bargain. "You've been lying to me," she told them (ICE agents had told her they were looking for a rapist in the area and then said they were searching for Paolo's former roommate), "and I've been lying to you. My husband's inside. I'm not letting you in, but we want a voluntary departure. We want 120 days." The agents agreed to leave, and Wendy and Paolo took a long and anguished drive to the federal building that afternoon. Thirty days later, Paolo was in Brazil. Wendy put their affairs in order, and then she went, too.

Paolo's family lives in a remote area of Brazil, formerly Amazon rainforest, without electricity, potable water, or paved roads. He and Wendy tried to make a living on the family's "meat cow" farm, with little success. They took antiparasitic medicine to avoid getting sick from the water. Wendy contracted dengue from a mosquito bite. "And it was just a tough place to live," she explained. Wendy and Paolo began looking into renting an apartment in Sao Paulo or Rio de Janeiro, but they found that even the smallest urban apartments in Brazil were far outside their price range.

Wendy's health deteriorated, and they began to be alarmed. They also struggled financially, and Wendy began to doubt the decision to interrupt her studies in the United States. After two difficult years, Wendy began considering a return to the United States to recuperate her health and finish her graduate degree. Paolo did not want her to leave, but he supported her decision, feeling guilty that she had sacrificed her health and career to stay with him. When they were alone together, he would tell her, "You are the only one making a sacrifice here. I'm not sacrificing." But the decision to leave Paolo was "tortuous," Wendy explained. "To have to make a decision between being with my husband or being healthy and having a healthy career. That just seemed very unfair."

Wendy did return to the United States to resume her graduate studies, and her physical health improved. But she suffered emotionally being away from Paolo. "To come back and be alone," she said, her narrative punctuated by sobs, "there is a deep loneliness that comes from being separated from my family, a deep yearning to be connected. And I know he's also [feeling] the same, telling me the house is so empty and so quiet. It's so difficult to be apart." When I talked with Wendy in 2013, they were planning to file an appeal to have Paolo's five-year bar reconsidered.

By 2015, they had given up hope. The appeal was "a waste of time and money," and they had to resign themselves to life apart. "I couldn't adapt to life in rural Brazil and he can't come here," Wendy explained. "We are planning to divorce, but I think we are both so sad about it and in shock that we haven't made any official moves forward." In the end, Wendy says, "The broken immigration system ruined our marriage."

Jorge and Beth

December 2006: Jorge was deported to Mexico, and neither he nor Beth was sure how to proceed. He headed to his mother's house on the outskirts of Mexico City, and Beth returned to Wisconsin, alone. While he was in the United States, Jorge had yearned to see his family in Mexico, but his deportation brought him shame, and he did not want his friends or family members to know that he had returned.[1] In addition, Jorge had difficulty adjusting to the living conditions in Mexico; although he had been sending money to his mom for home improvements over the years, her makeshift house still lacked running water and other things that he took for granted in his Wisconsin apartment. Back in Wisconsin, Beth went into a deep depression, ultimately deciding to put off graduate school to reunite with Jorge in Mexico.

February 2007: Beth moved to Mexico and found a job teaching English in Mexico City. Jorge found work in room service at a downtown hotel, and the couple eked out a living as they struggled to put together enough money to begin a consular processing/hardship waiver case. They talked about getting married and filing a family petition right away, but the processing time for spousal family petitions was long at the time—nearly two years. It would be more expedient, they thought, to begin immigration processing with an application for a fiancé visa. Beth filed the paperwork.

May 2007: Jorge's fiancé visa was approved, and they submitted a hardship petition to have his 10-year bar waived.

November 2007: As they waited for a decision on the waiver petition, Beth found out that she was pregnant. With a baby on the way, she took on a second job, also teaching English, and was commuting into Mexico City in the early morning, then returning to their home on the outskirts of the city in the afternoon, only to return to Mexico City in the evenings to teach again. Each morning, Beth would sit on the steps of a Mexico City subway station and hold her head in her hands in an attempt to control the waves of nausea caused by her morning sickness.

June 2008: Still waiting. Beth stopped working to take care of their newborn daughter. After weeks of living on one income and with her Mexican tourist visa set to expire, Beth decided to return to Wisconsin with their infant daughter and resume working in the United States. They expected an answer on the waiver petition soon anyway, and they made tentative plans to reunite in Wisconsin.

September 2008: Their hardship waiver petition was denied. The grounds for denial were based on another family's petition, and it was immediately clear that the adjudicator had made a mistake. Their attorney asked for reconsideration, and in October, Beth and Jorge received a second denial of the waiver petition on the grounds that Beth's hardship was not extreme enough to outweigh Jorge's "disrespect" for U.S. immigration laws. They filed another motion to reconsider.

December 2008: Beth and their daughter headed back to Mexico to be with Jorge as the appeal process dragged on.

March 2009: The denial of their waiver petition was upheld.

April 2009: Beth resumed teaching in Mexico City, and they left their infant daughter in the care of a neighbor while they were both at work. Their daughter began behaving strangely and having nightmares, and they were concerned that she was being abused. Beth quit her job to stay home with their daughter while Jorge put in as many hours as he could at the hotel.

November 2009: Tired of postponing their wedding, they borrowed $200 from Beth's mother and got married in a Mexico City courthouse.

December 2009: Unable to pay the attorney's fees that they needed to continue with their immigration case on Jorge's income alone, Beth and their daughter returned to Wisconsin so Beth could resume work there.

April 2010: They saved enough money to start the immigration process all over again, and Beth filed a family petition.

September 2010: Beth attended a marriage fraud interview in Wisconsin, and their family petition was approved shortly thereafter.

July 2011: Jorge went for his consular interview in Juárez, after which they submitted another hardship waiver petition.

February 2012: Their hardship waiver petition was referred. Beth made the decision to send their daughter to live with Jorge in Mexico so that she could work two jobs to support the family and keep their case going. She spent the next year and eight months working 60 hours per week and living without her husband and child.

August 2012: Their second waiver petition was denied on the grounds that Beth's hardship was not extreme and the relationship between Jorge and their daughter was "not clear."

November 2012: Tens of thousands of dollars in debt, discouraged, and having battled the immigration system for nearly six years, Beth and Jorge decided to give the waiver petition one last shot. Beth found a new lawyer, one who had gone to law school after working on her own husband's consular processing/hardship waiver case. The new lawyer redid their waiver petition to paint a stronger picture of Beth and Jorge's relationship and family, as well as Beth's suffering as a result of prolonged separation. This was their "hail Mary" pass, Beth said, their final try, and neither of them felt optimistic about the outcome.

May 2013: On Mother's Day, Beth called the National Visa Center on impulse, although she had promised herself to be patient and not torture herself by expecting an answer. The operator told her that Jorge's visa was being processed, and Beth began to sob. "No, this is good. This is good. You're approved," the operator explained. She did not understand that Beth was sobbing with relief. Beth hung up, then quickly called the center again to double-check that she had not misheard the operator and that the approval was real.

June 2013: The last time that Beth and I spoke over Skype, she was sitting in the kitchen of her Wisconsin home with Jorge puttering behind her, feeding the dog and periodically contributing to our interview.

They have adjusted to living together again quickly, they agree, although Beth worries that her relationship with her daughter is damaged from spending a year and a half apart. "There is a scar," Beth explained, "this sense of trauma about being separated, about knowing how quickly you can lose the people in your life. And even though it wasn't a permanent loss, it was a really awful thing to suddenly have someone just like ripped out of your life in just a day, you know? And so that—you carry it with you forever."

Life After Legalization

Lawful status has many benefits for formerly undocumented people. Perhaps most significant, it lessens the fear of deportation and allows people to move about safely, both locally and internationally, and be with family members on both sides of the border. Still, when the veil of living without papers lifts, the limits of legal status also come into sharper focus. For many, the relief of becoming legal is tempered by ongoing struggles with financial insecurity, relationship issues, entanglements with immigration authorities, and continued vulnerability to deportation.

Indeed, vulnerability to deportation only ends on naturalization as a U.S. citizen. Yet this process, too, is more onerous now than before. Pathways to citizenship that might have once existed are now partially replaced by a proliferation of provisional statuses that, together with lawful residency, confer a sense of legal legitimacy without any long-term security. I explore the implications of this trend next, in the concluding chapter.

CHAPTER 7

Documented and Deportable

René and Molly

"It's been like Christmas at our house all week," Molly laughs, watching as René extracts his new driver license from his wallet to show me. I surmise that it is not the first time that René has shown it off. It's the spring of 2015, and there has been some movement for René and his family on the immigration horizon.

First, in January 2013, the Illinois governor signed a bill that allows undocumented residents of the state to obtain driver licenses. Illinois is one of a growing number of U.S. states to enact such a bill, which helps shield drivers like René from deportations that result from traffic stops.

Then, in November 2014 (on my birthday, to be exact), President Obama announced that his administration would implement a program called Deferred Action for Parental Accountability, or DAPA. DAPA is modeled on DACA, the deferred action for youth implemented by the Obama administration in 2012. DAPA is intended to benefit undocumented parents of U.S.-citizen and lawfully resident children who have lived in the United States continuously since 2010 and who are not otherwise a priority for deportation. In most cases, this refers to parents of U.S. citizens who have no serious criminal record. Like DACA, DAPA is neither lawful residency nor a pathway to lawful residency, but a temporary work permit and a promise not to pursue deportation at this time.

DAPA was going to be implemented in the spring of 2015, but it has been held up in court. Twenty-six states have brought a lawsuit against the Obama administration to stop DAPA, which is turning into the latest casualty in an ongoing battle between states' rights and federal power, between the political "right" and "left." René and Molly care little about the partisan bickering. They and their children just want to stay together.

As they watch the news on immigration closely, René and Molly join an estimated 4 to 5 million families who would benefit from DAPA but are being held in suspense, waiting for a decision. Waiting for something.

In this book, I have traced the steps of mixed-status families as they try to secure lawful status for an undocumented loved one. I have shown how most families find their way blocked early on by a minefield of obstacles: they do not have the right kind of family, or family members do not have the right kind of citizenship, or the applicant has an immigration or criminal record that makes him or her ineligible, or the family cannot afford it, or they are simply not willing to risk denial and indefinite separation or relocation. Even the lucky few who undertake immigration processing successfully find the process burdensome and degrading because it robs them of the autonomy to decide where, and with whom, they can live their lives. In this process, relationships are undermined, children are traumatized, families go broke, and the vast majority of undocumented people in the United States remain undocumented.

It is not surprising that many people describe this system as broken. Certainly, for Wendy and Paolo, Jorge and Beth, Luis, Veronica, Anya and Enrique, and all of the other people whom I interviewed, the system is broken or at least severely malfunctioning. The claim that the U.S. immigration system is broken has wide currency and has driven recent proposals for immigration reform in the nation's capitol. Yet, more often than not, these proposals maintain or enhance the cruelest and most expensive components of the immigration system, further undermining families. The persistence of the system and nature of the fixes thus raise an important question: Is the system broken? And, if so, for whom? In this brief conclusion, I consider how to make sense of an immigration system that purports to prioritize family unity yet tears mixed-status families apart or leaves them suspended in a prolonged state of uncertainty.

Making Sense of a Broken System

It is important to note that although the immigration system is dysfunctional for millions of people in mixed-status families, for many other people the "broken" system works just fine. In fact, thousands of U.S. employers, industries, and agencies benefit from unauthorized migration and the massive enforcement apparatus that has been built up around it.

With a labor force participation rate around 94 percent, undocumented men are among the most active members of the U.S. work force (Passel and Cohn 2009). Undocumented workers earn less, are more likely to live in poverty, and are less likely to have health insurance and other benefits than their documented counterparts (Kochhar 2005; Mehta et al. 2002). The vulnerability of undocumented workers makes them an especially profitable and desirable labor force for low-paying U.S. employers (De Genova 2005; Gomberg-Muñoz 2011; Heyman 2001; Zlolniski 2006), who lobby hard to maintain access to this work force (see, e.g., Welna 2013). Undocumented workers are especially concentrated in agriculture, manufacturing, and low-end service work (Horton 2016; Passel and Cohn 2009), where their underpaid labor subsidizes the prices that U.S. consumers pay for food, goods, and services.

Undocumented workers also pay billions of tax dollars that flow into Social Security and Medicaid coffers for benefits that they cannot claim. A 2014 report by the Institute on Taxation and Economic Policy found that undocumented people paid nearly $12 billion in federal, state, and local taxes in 2012 alone, at an average effective tax rate of 8 percent (compare this to the effective tax rate of 5.4 percent paid by the top 1 percent of U.S. taxpayers) (Gardner et al. 2015). Despite these contributions, undocumented workers are ineligible for Social Security, Medicare, health care under the Affordable Care Act, unemployment benefits, federal housing programs, food stamps, Supplemental Security Income, Temporary Assistance for Needy Families, most Medicaid services, and Earned Income Tax Credit. In fact, the only public services that undocumented people are eligible to use are emergency medical care under the Medicaid system and elementary and secondary public education. The result is likely a net gain for the U.S. economy— in fact, a national survey of leading economists found that 85 percent agreed that undocumented immigrants have a positive (74 percent) or neutral (11 percent) impact on the U.S. economy (Lipman 2006).

Agencies and industries tasked with "securing" the nation from undocumented people also reap the benefits of a broken system (Golash-Boza 2009). The budget for immigration enforcement in the

United States has skyrocketed since the 1980s, when the buildup of border policing began in earnest. The U.S. federal government spent nearly $12 billion on border security in 2012 alone (Dwoskin 2013), the overwhelming majority of which was concentrated on the U.S. border with Mexico. Immigration expenditures reflect government priorities: between 1986 and 2002, funding for the U.S. Border Patrol grew more than 300 percent, whereas funding for detention and removal grew more than 800 percent (Dixon and Gelatt 2005). In contrast, funding for consular affairs, which would help alleviate the backlog of visa applications and prolonged consular processing times, increased by a meager 8 percent (Dixon and Gelatt 2005).

Increasingly, immigration enforcement dollars are routed into the bank accounts of private prison corporations. ICE spends about $2 billion annually to detain immigrants, most of which is paid to one of two private prison corporations, the GEO Group or Corrections Corporation of America (CCA). In fact, nearly two-thirds of the more than 30,000 immigrants held in detention each day are in facilities owned by either GEO or CCA (Selway and Newkirk 2013). In 2012 alone, CCA earned $752 million in revenue from federal contracts, $206 million of which came from ICE (Selway and Newkirk 2013). The private corporations that hold immigration contracts spend tens of millions of dollars on political lobbying and have been major campaign contributors to immigration hard-liners (Selway and Newkirk 2013; Sullivan 2010). In return, Congress has mandated that 34,000 people be kept in immigrant detention, including children, every day. In these detention centers, tens of thousands of detained immigrants continue to work, providing essential labor to the centers' operations for $1 a day or less. In 2013, more than 60,000 immigrants worked while they were detained, making the centers, together, the single largest employer of immigrant workers in the nation (Urbina 2014).

Interestingly, private prison corporations may also be benefiting from immigration enforcement in an indirect way: through "leasing" prison inmates for work in areas targeted by immigration enforcement measures. Bruce Farely, manager of the business development unit of Arizona Correctional Industries, says that they are "contacted almost daily" by companies that "are looking to inmate labor as a possible alternative" to undocumented labor (in Watkins 2011). Labor shortages in the agricultural sector brought on by a reduction of the undocumented labor force have led growers to seek prison labor in Arizona, Colorado, and Idaho (Battey 2007; Univision 2009). There is political support for this practice: in 2011, the Georgia governor Nathan Deal said that filling available jobs with people on criminal probation is "a great partial solution" to labor shortages in the agricultural sector resulting from the state's restrictive immigration policy (Shoichet 2011).

Enforcement funding is funneled not only into more personnel, detention centers, and sophisticated technology, but also into massive infrastructure projects, such as the fence that lines more than 600 miles of the U.S.–Mexico border. The Government Accountability Office estimated that the pedestrian border fence built by DHS between 2007 and 2008 cost the agency an average of $3.9 million *per mile* in construction contracts (U.S. Government Accountability Office 2009). Immigration reform legislation passed in the U.S. Senate in 2013 proposed extending the border fence an additional 700 miles, at an estimated cost of $28 billion dollars (Dwoskin 2013). Yet, with all of this "security," the U.S.–Mexico border is deadlier than ever because the border fence reroutes migrants into ever more dangerous territory. On average, the trek through the U.S.–Mexico border region now kills nearly one person every day (U.S. Customs and Border Protection 2014).

In addition to all of the financial revenue generated by massive expenditures on immigration enforcement and security, the immigration system also generates political capital. Politicians in both major parties benefit from fanning the flames of immigration passions to win votes from constituents (Golash-Boza 2009), as well as from campaign donations made by the companies that profit from immigrant detention and border militarization (Selway and Newkirk 2013). In this context, it is perhaps not surprising that political winds seem to blow in favor of stagnation on immigration reform or toward policies that only reproduce the flaws of a broken system.

In sum, calling the U.S. immigration system "broken" makes it sound like an accident. It is not. U.S. immigration policies are carefully designed, well funded, and forcefully carried out by legislators and government agencies. Disagreement among lawmakers and government actors generates modifications to U.S. immigration law, but overall, the system works largely as intended: it excludes some and includes others in a matter consistent with the prevailing ideologies and political economy of the nation-state.

Precarity as Policy

Despite their myriad benefits to certain sectors of the U.S. population, millions of people who live somewhat outside the purview of the state do potentially pose a problem for security agendas. Rather than reducing this population through an amnesty program such as the one passed by the Ronald Reagan administration in 1986, contemporary policies signal a shift in strategy: the proliferation of provisional immigration statuses (Menjívar and Kanstroom 2014).

Provisional immigration statuses are not entirely new to U.S. immigration programs: by 1990, Congress had agreed to grant temporary protected status to select Central Americans, which would temporarily shield them from deportation without conferring any permanent lawful standing, creating a "liminal legality" in which hundreds of thousands of Central Americans became trapped (Menjívar 2006). And in the 1990s, even as the border between the United States and Mexico was being militarized, temporary visas for certain high-skill workers were being created (Leiden and Neal 1990). Today, hundreds of thousands of immigrant workers are contracted annually as "guest workers" who fill positions in agriculture, information technology, science, and medicine (Banerjee 2010; Batalova 2010). And even "high-skilled" guest workers share some of the vulnerabilities of their bracero-era counterparts, including having their legal status tied to a particular employer, vulnerability to exploitative pay and working conditions, and a tenuous status that renders their work situations highly unpredictable and insecure over the long term (Banerjee 2010). Thus, although temporary visa holders escape the criminalization that targets undocumented people, they remain "documented but marginalized" in their U.S. jobs (Banerjee 2010).

Recently, the scale of provisional statuses has increased by way of two "executive actions," launched by the Executive Branch but not legislated through Congress. In 2012, the Barack Obama administration implemented DACA. DACA allows unauthorized youth who arrived in the United States when they were 16 years old or younger, and who have graduated from or are enrolled in high school, to apply for a two-year deferral of deportation and work permit. In 2014, the administration announced that it would extend DACA eligibility to three years and implement DAPA, which extends the benefits of DACA to certain parents of U.S. citizens, like René. Although these programs can potentially provide relief for some 7 million undocumented people, they are also limited in scope, scale, and duration.

First, even if DAPA goes into effect, millions of undocumented people in the United States—some 6 to 7 million—will not qualify for either DACA or DAPA. Among them are people who are childless (including many lesbian, gay, bisexual, transgender, and queer people), parents whose children are also undocumented or DACA eligible, anyone with a "serious" criminal record (possibly including convictions for unlawful reentry), and anyone who cannot prove continuous residence since 2010 (for DAPA). The latter criterion is especially onerous for cyclical migrants and people who work in the informal economy (such as off-the-books domestic work) and may especially burden immigrant women.

The benefits provided by these programs are also limited. DACA/DAPA eligibility does not guarantee protection from deportation, but rather the use of prosecutorial discretion in a deportation case—a big difference. And even with work eligibility, program participants will still not qualify for most public benefits, including health care under the Affordable Care Act, Supplemental Security Income, Medicaid (except for emergency care), Temporary Assistance for Needy Families, or the Supplemental Nutrition Assistance Program, although workers pay into those programs with their tax dollars. Finally, neither DACA nor DAPA is either lawful permanent residency or a path to lawful permanent residency—it is merely a promise not to pursue deportation at this time. The economic and political vulnerabilities of program participants may be reduced, but they will persist.

Finally, the duration of these programs is limited—eligibility is only good for two (DACA) or three (expanded DACA and DAPA) years. At the end of that period, participants may be able to reapply if the program is still available; but executive action is not legislation, and it can be ended at any time. In the meantime, those who remain eligible will be held in an indefinite state of legal precarity or, as Cecilia Menjívar (2006) puts it, liminal legality, which confers on them some legal recognition without any long-term security. Together, DACA and DAPA, along with temporary protected status, create a subclass of millions of U.S. immigrants who are neither fully legal nor illegal but who are registered with the state and subject to routine state surveillance (Menjívar 2006).

Liminal legality is not limited to executive actions; it has found its way into proposed legislation as well. Most recently, the immigration bill that passed in the U.S. Senate in 2013 (but was not taken up in the House) included a legalization program for some undocumented people. In the last iteration of the Senate bill, undocumented people would need to satisfy a battery of criteria to be eligible for the legalization program, including "continuous employment," an average income above the federal poverty level, and payment of costly fees and penalties. And program participants would be required to continually satisfy these criteria for 15 years or more. During this time, they would hold a provisional status, much like parole, in which their movement would be restricted and their behavior monitored closely. Those who lose eligibility during the provisional period would become subject to detention and deportation, joining an estimated 4 to 5 million people who are not expected to qualify for the legalization program in the first place. Those who do remain eligible for the extended provisional period would eventually be able to apply for legal permanent U.S. residency and, after several more years, U.S. citizenship (†S 744 ES).

It is interesting to note that the legalization program was wrapped in the language of "national security." For example, the head of DHS at the time, Janet Napolitano, said that the legalization program would enhance national security by "bring[ing] people out of the shadows" so that "we know who they are. We know where they are" (quoted in Fox News Latino 2013). The Republican senator and former vice-presidential candidate Paul Ryan agreed that legalization is vital, "to know which individuals are in the country illegally for national security reasons" (James 2013), adding on his website that, with legalization, "now we will know who they are." Although it may be tempting to view these statements as cynical attempts to drum up political support for the bill among conservatives, I believe that viewing legalization as an important component of state security agendas is both fruitful and illuminating.

The effects of such legislation on the U.S. undocumented population would be manifold. First, it would bring millions of undocumented people "out of the shadows" and into the waiting embrace of the state, where they would be fingerprinted, registered, and either detained and deported or surveilled and regulated for a prolonged and indefinite period. Second, it would further institutionalize distinctions between more and less "deserving" immigrants based on criteria that are especially related to race, gender, and class. Third, it would force undocumented people, especially women, into the U.S. work force in ever-larger numbers to satisfy employment and income criteria. Finally, it would shift the risks of deportation from random and unpredictable encounters with immigration enforcement to a pervasive and routine surveillance by agents of the state. Together with the continued vulnerability of lawful permanent residents that I described in Chapter 6, provisional statuses signal an expansion of a U.S. immigrant population that is both documented and deportable.

Making Law Visible

This book has shown how the U.S. immigration system relegates undocumented people and their family members to a life of indefinite uncertainty. This is most obvious in massive enforcement campaigns that have resulted in the detention and deportation of millions of people, many of whom leave behind broken families that struggle with the loss of partners and parents. Yet, it is also apparent in the criteria for legalization, which all but guarantee that most undocumented people in the United States will stay that way, and in the proliferation of provisional statuses that bring people under the purview of state control without removing their vulnerability to deportation.

Still, there are those who argue that the contemporary immigration regime is fair, or even generous, in that the modicum of protection offered by intermediate statuses amounts to a reward for people who, with their very presence, have broken U.S. law. Leaving aside for the moment the obvious objection that U.S.-citizen family members of undocumented people have broken no such laws and yet also suffer from the immigration system, let us consider the "illegality" of undocumented people in this final section.

In Chapter 2, I posed two questions. One was "Is contemporary immigration policy and practice race neutral?" Throughout this book, I have presented evidence that contemporary immigration policy and practice is not race neutral but deeply shaped by stereotyping and criminalization of Latino men. The other question was "Is immigration status a more legitimate basis for discrimination and exclusion today than race was in the past?"

Certainly, the notion that "illegal" is "illegal" and, therefore, that subjugation, detention, and deportation of undocumented people is both neutral and morally justifiable, has wide popular currency. According to this perspective, exclusion based on immigration status is fundamentally different from exclusion based on race because it results from the "law-breaking" behavior of individuals. Thus, it is what people "do," their violation of law, and not what they "are," their racial classification, which determines how they are treated under the law. This rendering of immigration law makes it appear both fair and impartial.

But this perspective reduces unauthorized migration to the actions of migrants, overlooking the role of law in sanctioning some border crossings and criminalizing others. Migration is only illegal when laws prevent mobility. Every day when I go to work, I cross a city border, yet that crossing is not illegal because that border is not restricted. For me, even policed borders largely do not hinder my mobility. As a U.S. citizen, I visit Mexico at least once a year; I can travel back and forth freely. I do not even need a visa. I have never undergone a travel-related physical exam or biometrics check, and security agents at the airport have never interrogated me. The "law" sanctions my uninhibited travel because of the mere fact of my birth in the United States. There is nothing given or necessarily fair about this.

FIGURE 7.1 Empathy, the Mexican side of the border fence. Photograph by Steve Pavey, Hope in Focus Photography. www.stevepavey.com/.

Indeed, much like racial categories, the distinction between legal and illegal migration is a cultural invention that has been (as racial categories were) codified in law. And legal codification alone does not make a practice morally legitimate, much less socially just; only consider that *racial exclusion was explicitly legal* until the 1960s. (Moreover, U.S. foreign and economic policies violate national borders and state sovereignty via military invasion and trade policies all the time, so why are migrants punished for doing it?) Reducing undocumented migration to the behaviors of migrants and ignoring how law structures migration patterns is not merely overly simplistic; it also distorts the relations of power that shape a person's status in society, renders law invisible and unassailable, and legitimizes inequality by dismissing claims to resources and rights made by disempowered people.

In contrast, an attention to processes that illegalize migration, as Nicholas De Genova (2002, 2005) has argued, illuminates the role of law in creating both legality and illegality. This is apparent not only in policies that are explicitly exclusionary or restrictionist, but also in programs that govern inclusion, such as the family-based processing that I have described here. Attention to how immigration policies are created, enacted, and experienced "on the ground" allows us to read policy making as a dynamic cultural process that is deeply embedded in broader sociopolitical and economic contexts.

When we do, it becomes apparent that the process I describe in this book is not a broken part of a broken system, much less a faulty part in an otherwise functioning one. Rather, like most structures of exclusion, the U.S. immigration system works for some and not for others; indeed, it benefits some at the expense of others. As Lourdes put it, "I guess what I'm trying to say is that it just really sucks how all this stuff works. . . . I was basically part of sending three black youth to a juvenile detention because they were the people that beat up my brother [making her family eligible for a U visa]. It's one of those things where, if I connect the dots and I really see how things happen, I realize that we're all just pawns in this game."

Group One

Seeking Status Change, Ineligible for Family-Based Processing

Name (U.S.-citizen spouse)	Year of first entry to United States	Mode of entry	Country of birth	Process	Status as of June 2014	Chapter(s)
Felipe	1997	EWI	Mexico	Removal	Deported, living in Mexico (family in United States)	
Isabel	1988	EWI	Mexico	NA	Undocumented	
Juan	1995	EWI	Mexico	NA	Undocumented	1, 3
Lily (Carl)*	1995	EWI	Mexico	Removal/ DACA	DACA recipient	3
Lourdes	2001	EWI	Mexico	U visa	Conditional residency	3, 6, 7
Luis	1995	EWI	Mexico	DACA	DACA recipient	3, 6
María	1999	EWI	Mexico	U visa	Conditional residency	6
Noe (Kaitlin)	1996	EWI	Mexico	NA	Undocumented	3, 5
Pancho	1980	EWI	Mexico	NA	Undocumented	
Raymundo	1957	Bracero visa	Mexico	NA	Undocumented	
René (Molly)	1995	EWI	Mexico	NA	Undocumented	1, 3, 6, 7
Roberto	1995	EWI	Mexico	NA	Undocumented	
Rosa	1999	EWI	Mexico	NA	Undocumented	
Sam	1994	EWI	Mexico	DACA	DACA recipient	6

continued

Name (U.S.-citizen spouse)	Year of first entry to United States	Mode of entry	Country of birth	Process	Status as of June 2014	Chapter(s)
Sara	1999	Tourist visa	Ecuador	NA	Undocumented	
Sofia	1997	EWI	Mexico	Removal; suspension of deportation	Undocumented	
Yari	1994	Tourist visa	Mexico	DACA	DACA recipient	

DACA, Deferred Action for Childhood Arrivals; EWI, entry without inspection; NA, not applicable.
*Lily is eligible to seek residency through her U.S. citizen husband under the law, but she is unable to do so because of the uncertainty of the outcome.

Group Two
Undertook Family-Based Immigration Processing

Name (U.S.- citizen petitioner)	Year of first entry to United States	Mode of entry	Country of birth	Process	Status as of June 2014	Time in processing	Chapter(s)
Abril (stepfather)	1989	EWI	Mexico	Adjustment of status	U.S. citizen	10 years	3, 6
Alberto (Heather)	1998	EWI	Mexico	Removal/ consular processing	Living apart	7 years, still in processing	4, 5
Beto (Christine)	1996	Tourist visa	Bolivia	Removal/ consular processing	Living together in Bolivia	4 years	4
Carlos (Grace)	1996	EWI	Mexico	Consular processing	LPR	18 months	5, 6
Cuautemoc (Nayeli)	1999	EWI	Mexico	Consular processing with provisional waiver	Un- documented	1 year, still in processing	
Enrique (Anya)	1998	EWI	Mexico	Consular processing	LPR	18 months	1, 2, 3, 4, 5, 6
Leticia (spouse)	1997	EWI	Mexico	Consular processing	U.S. citizen	1 year	6
Gio (Rosie)	2002	Tourist visa	Mexico	Adjustment of status	LPR	6 months	4
Guillermo (Marie)	1994	EWI	Mexico	Consular processing	U.S. citizen	1 year	5, 6
Gume (husband)	1989	EWI	Mexico	Adjustment of status	LPR	6 months	6
Hector (Cynthia)	1992	EWI	Mexico	Consular processing	LPR	2 years	3, 5, 6

continued

Name (U.S.-citizen petitioner)	Year of first entry to United States	Mode of entry	Country of birth	Process	Status as of June 2014	Time in processing	Chapter(s)
Isaiah (Jane)	2005	EWI	Mexico	Consular processing	Waiver denied, living together in Mexico	2 years	5, 6
Javier (Stephanie)	2007	EWI	Mexico	Consular processing with provisional waiver	LPR	1 year	5, 6
Jorge (Beth)	2000	EWI	Mexico	Removal/ consular processing	LPR	6 years	3, 5, 6
Lorelei (parents)	1980	Tourist visa	Mexico	Adjustment of status	LPR	1 year	
Lucy (sibling)	1996	Tourist visa	Colombia	Adjustment of status	LPR	10 years	6
Lupita (Ramón)	1992	EWI	Mexico	Consular processing	Permanent bar, living in Mexico	1 year	4
Manuel (Danielle)	2003	EWI	El Salvador	Removal/ consular processing	LPR	3 years	5
Marco (Tanya)	1990	EWI	Mexico	Consular processing	Conditional visa	2 years	3, 4, 5, 6
Nico (Natalie)	2005	EWI	Honduras	Removal/ consular processing	5-year unwaivable bar, living apart	5 years, still in processing	4, 5
Paolo (Wendy)	2004 or 2005	EWI	Brazil	Removal/ consular processing	5-year unwaivable bar, living apart	4 years	4, 5, 6
Pepe (Rachel)	2009	Fiancé visa	Nicaragua	Adjustment of status	LPR	1 year	
Rosita (husband)	1996	EWI	Mexico	Adjustment of status	U.S. citizen	6 months	6
Veronica (Francisco)	2008	Tourist visa	Mexico	Adjustment of status	Conditional visa	3 years	3, 6
Victor (Pamela)	1994	EWI	Mexico	Consular processing	LPR	18 months	4, 5, 6

EWI, entry without inspection; LPR, lawful permanent resident.

TERMINOLOGY

....

I use terminology in this book that warrants some discussion. Consistent with popular and academic usage, I use "undocumented" to refer to people who do not have a temporary visa, legal permanent residency, or citizenship in the nation-state where they live. The term undocumented is something of a misnomer, since undocumented people can and do possess both valid and invalid identity documents. Still, undocumented avoids the pejorative connotation of "illegal" (itself a legal misnomer), is more widely understood than "unauthorized," and is the term that my study participants prefer.

I also describe my foreign-born study participants as "immigrants" rather than "migrants" or "transmigrants." As Nicholas De Genova (2005) has pointed out, "immigrant" and "immigration" always reflect the perspective of the receiving nation-state and, thus, are inherently nationalist. Moreover, "immigrant" presupposes legal admission to the nation-state and, thus, "undocumented immigrant" and "illegal immigrant" are technically contradictions in terms (Plascencia 2009). Even so, "migrant" and "transmigrant" imply transience and mobility, and my study participants are settled in the United States for the long term and, indeed, are striving to become lawful U.S. immigrants.

I use the term "mixed-status family" to describe any self-identified family that consists of any combination of undocumented people with lawful residents and/or U.S. citizens. The term family has the advantage of being widely understood to describe relationships of ancestry and marriage, but it is also criticized as a concept that validates only certain kinds of relationships and, thus, reproduces heteropatriarchal power structures and middle-class norms. Here, I use family to mean people who feel like they belong to each other (Sahlins 2013), although, as I also discuss, eligibility for U.S. immigration processing is predicated on legally sanctioned relationships and excludes many kinds of families. I deviate slightly from the Pew Hispanic Center's definition of a mixed-status family. Demographers at Pew use mixed-status family to refer only to families that consist of at least one undocumented adult and at least one U.S.-citizen child; I use it more broadly here to mean any self-defined family that consists of people with different immigration and/or citizenship statuses.

LIST OF ABBREVIATIONS

....

CIMT: Crimes involving moral turpitude

DACA: Deferred Action for Childhood Arrivals

DAPA: Deferred Action for Parental Accountability

DHS: U.S. Department of Homeland Security

ICE: U.S. Immigration and Customs Enforcement

IIRAIRA: Illegal Immigration Reform and Immigrant
Responsibility Act

INA: Immigration and Nationality Act

IRCA: Immigration Reform and Control Act

NAFTA: North American Free Trade Agreement

NVC: National Visa Center

USCIS: U.S. Citizenship and Immigration Services

Chapter 1

1. http://www.dhs.gov/i-601-waivers-inadmissibility-does-current-process-work-when-hardship-extreme-do-alternative-models/.
2. There is a third program, 245(i) adjustment, which applies to undocumented people whose family members filed an approvable petition on their behalf on or before April 30, 2001. Since no one with whom I spoke qualified under 245(i), I do not discuss it at length here.
3. Certain USCIS instructions include children older than 21 as potential petitioners for waivers of bars of inadmissibility; however, adult children were not considered eligible petitioners in any of the cases that I followed.

Chapter 2

1. Given the demand for U.S. visas, Enrique had a better chance at winning the lottery. If he did win the lottery, he could take advantage of another, lesser-known, immigration program, which offers U.S. immigrant visas in exchange for a $500,000 "investment."

Chapter 3

1. Lawful permanent residents can petition for their undocumented spouses and children, but they are subject to annual caps and must wait in line for a visa to become available.

Chapter 4

1. See Plascencia (2009).
2. Between 1994 and 2001, Congress periodically "opened" a provision in the law that allowed unlawful entrants to adjust without leaving, but this provision has been "closed" since April 30, 2001 (Immigrant Legal Resource Center 2012).

Chapter 5

1. One young woman, Emily Bonderer Cruz, blogs as "The Real Housewife of Ciudad Juárez." She poignantly addresses these attacks in a blog post entitled "25 Things I Love about My Ham Sandwich": http://therealhouse wifeofciudadjuarez.blogspot.com/2011/07/25-things-i-love-about-my-ham-sandwich.html/.

Chapter 6

1. Jorge's embarrassment is understandable: the prevailing assumption in Mexico and elsewhere is that only people convicted of serious crimes are deported from the United States, and deportees are widely stigmatized as criminals there (Coutin 2007).

REFERENCES

Abrego, Leisy
2014   *Sacrificing Families: Navigating Laws, Labor, and Love across Borders.*
        Stanford, CA: Stanford University Press.

Abrego, Leisy, and Cecilia Menjívar
2011   Immigrant Latina Mothers as Targets of Legal Violence. *International
        Journal of Sociology of the Family* 37(1): 9–26.

Alexander, Michelle
2010   *The New Jim Crow: Mass Incarceration in the Age of Colorblindness.*
        New York: New Press.

American Immigration Council
2014   *Reagan–Bush Family Fairness: A Chronological History.* Washington,
        DC: American Immigration Council.

Balderrama, Francisco E., and Raymond Rodriguez
2006   *Decade of Betrayal: Mexican Repatriation in the 1930s.* Albuquerque:
        University of New Mexico Press.

Banerjee, P.
2010   Transnational Subcontracting, Indian IT Workers, and the U.S. Visa
        System. *Women's Studies Quarterly* 38(1/2): 89–111.

Basch, Linda, Nina Glick Schiller, and Cristina Szanton Blanc
1994   *Nations Unbound: Transnational Projects, Postcolonial Predicaments,
        and Deterritorialized Nation-States.* Amsterdam: Gordon & Breach.

Batalova, Jeanne
2010   *H-1B Temporary Skilled Worker Program.* Migration Policy Institute.
         October 7. http://www.migrationpolicy.org/article/h-1b-temporary-
         skilled-worker-program/, accessed July 25, 2015.

Battey, Allison
2007   *Facing Illegal Immigrant Crackdown, Farms Look to Inmate Labor.*
         ABC News, July 25. http://abcnews.go.com/ThcLaw/story?id=
         3409570&page=1/, retrieved June 4, 2011.

Baum, Jonathan, Rosha Jones, and Catherine Barry
2010   *In the Child's Best Interests? The Consequences of Losing a Lawful
         Immigrant Parent to Deportation.* Berkeley and Davis: International
         Human Rights Law Clinic, Chief Justice Earl Warren Institute on
         Race, Ethnicity and Diversity, and Immigration Law Clinic.

Blackmon, Douglas
2009   *Slavery by Another Name: The Re-Enslavement of Black Americans
         from the Civil War to World War II.* New York: Anchor Books.

Boehm, Deborah
2012   *Intimate Migrations: Gender, Family, and Illegality among
         Transnational Mexicans.* New York: New York University Press.

Bosniak, Linda
2006   *The Citizen and the Alien: Dilemmas of Contemporary Membership.*
         Princeton, NJ: Princeton University Press.

Bourgois, Philippe, and Jeffrey Schonberg
2009   *Righteous Dopefiend.* Berkeley: University of California Press.

Brotherton, David, and Luis Barrios
2011   *Banished to the Homeland: Dominican Deportees and Their Stories of
         Exile.* New York: Columbia University Press.

Cacho, Lisa Marie
2012   *Social Death: Racialized Rightlessness and the Criminalization of the
         Unprotected.* New York: New York University Press.

Calavita, Kitty
1994   U.S. Immigration and Policy Responses: The Limits of Legislation.
         In *Controlling Immigration,* edited by Wayne Cornelius, Philip Martin,
         and James Hollifield. Stanford, CA: Stanford University Press.

Cardoso, Lawrence A.
1980   *Mexican Emigration to the United States 1987–1931.* Tucson: University
         of Arizona Press.

Castañeda, Heide, and Milena Andrea Melo
2014   Health Care Access for Latino Mixed-Status Families: Barriers,
        Strategies and Implications for Reform. *American Behavioral Scientist*
        58(14): 1891–1909.

Chacon, Justin Akers, and Mike Davis
2006   *No One Is Illegal: Fighting Racism and State Violence on the U.S.–Mexico
        Border.* Chicago: Haymarket Books.

Chang, Grace
2000   *Disposable Domestics: Immigrant Women Workers in the Global
        Economy.* Cambridge, UK: South End Press.

Chavez, Leo
2008   *The Latino Threat: Constructing Immigrants, Citizens, and the Nation.*
        Stanford, CA: Stanford University Press.
1992   *Shadowed Lives: Undocumented Immigrants in American Society.*
        New York: Wadsworth.
1988   Settlers and Sojourners: The Case of Mexicans in the United States.
        Human Organization 47(2): 95–108.

CNN World
2010   *U.S. Weapons Fuel Drug Violence, Mexico's President Says.* CNN
        World. September 11, 2010. http://www.cnn.com/2010/WORLD/
        americas/09/11/mexico.president.interview/, accessed August 6, 2014.

Coutin, Susan Bibler
2007   *Nation of Emigrants: Shifting Boundaries of Citizenship in El Salvador
        and the United States.* New York: Cornell University Press.
2003   Suspension of Deportation Hearings and Measures of "Americanness."
        The Journal of Latin American Anthropology 8(2): 8–95.
2000a   *Legalizing Moves: Salvadoran Immigrants' Struggle for U.S. Residency.*
        Ann Arbor: University of Michigan Press.
2000b   Denationalization, Inclusion, and Exclusion: Negotiating the Boundaries
        of Belonging. *Indiana Journal of Global Legal Studies* 7(2): 585–593.

Daniels, Roger
2001   Two Cheers for Immigration. In *Debating American Immigration,
        1882–Present.* Roger Daniels and Otis L. Graham. New York: Rowman &
        Littlefield.

De Genova, Nicholas
2010   The Deportation Regime: Sovereignty, Space, and the Freedom of
        Movement. In *The Deportation Regime: Sovereignty, Space, and the*

Freedom of Movement, edited by Nicholas De Genova and Nathalie Peutz. Durham, NC: Duke University Press.

2005   *Working the Boundaries: Race, Space, and "Illegality" in Mexican Chicago*. Durham, NC: Duke University Press.

2004   The Legal Production of Mexican/Migrant "Illegality." *Latino Studies* 2: 160–185.

2002   Migrant Illegality and Deportability in Everyday Life. *Annual Review of Anthropology* 31: 419–447.

De Genova, Nicholas, and Ana Y. Ramos-Zayas
2003   *Latino Crossings: Mexicans, Puerto Ricans, and the Politics of Race and Citizenship*. New York: Routledge.

De León, Jason
2015   *The Land of Open Graves: Living and Dying on the Migrant Trail*. Berkeley: University of California Press.

Delgado Wise, Raúl, and James Cypher
2007   The Strategic Role of Mexican Labor under NAFTA: Critical Perspectives on Current Economic Integration. *Annals of the American Academy of Political and Social Science* 610(1): 119–142.

Detention Watch Network
2014   *End the Immigration Detention Bed Quota*. Washington, DC: Detention Watch Network. http://www.detentionwatchnetwork.org/EndTheQuotaNarrative/, accessed July 24, 2015.

Dixon, David, and Julia Gelatt
2005   *Immigration Enforcement Spending since IRCA*. Washington, DC: Migration Policy Institute.

Dreby, Joanna
2015   *Everyday Illegal: When Policies Undermine Immigrant Families*. Berkeley: University of California Press.

2012   The Burden of Deportation on Children in Mexican Immigrant Families. *Journal of Marriage and Family* 74: 829–845.

Dwoskin, Elizabeth
2013   Sealing the U.S. Border Would Cost an Additional $28 Billion a Year. *Bloomberg Business, Policy*. March 13.

Enchautegui, Maria, and Cecilia Menjívar
2015   Paradoxes of Family Immigration Policy: Separation, Reorganization, and Reunification of Families under Current Immigration Laws. *Law & Policy* 37(1–2): 32–60.

Fix, Michael, and Wendy Zimmerman
2001   All under One Roof: Mixed-Status Families in an Era of Reform. *International Migration Review* 35(2): 397–419.

Fox News Latino
2013   Janet Napolitano Dismissed Critics, Insisted New Immigration Law Would Boost National Security. *Politics.* April 24.

Fussell, Elizabeth
2011   The Deportation Threat Dynamic and Victimization of Latino Migrants: Wage Theft and Robbery. *The Sociological Quarterly* 52(4): 593–615.

Gardner, Matthew, Sebastian Johnson, and Meg Wiehe
2015   *Undocumented Immigrants' State and Local Tax Contributions.* Washington, DC: Institute on Taxation and Economic Policy.

Gardner, T., II, and A. Kohli
2009   *The C.A.P. Effect: Racial Profiling in the ICE Criminal Alien Program.* Policy Brief. Berkeley: Chief Justice Earl Warren Institute on Race, Ethnicity & Diversity Berkeley Law Center for Research and Administration. http://www.warreninstitute.org/, accessed September 19, 2014.

Gerken, Cristina
2013   *Model Immigrants and Undesirable Aliens: The Cost of Immigration Reform in the 1990s.* Minneapolis: University of Minnesota Press.

Golash-Boza, Tanya
2015   *Deported: Policing Immigrants, Disposable Labor, and Global Capitalism.* New York: New York University Press.
2012a   *Due Process Denied: Detentions and Deportations in the United States.* New York: Routledge.
2012b   *Immigration Nation: Raids, Detentions, and Deportations in Post 9/11 America.* New York: Paradigm.
2009   A Confluence of Interests in Immigration Enforcement: How Politicians, the Media, and Corporations Profit from Immigration Policies Destined to Fail. *Sociology Compass* 3: 293–294.

Golash-Boza, Tanya, and Pierrette Hondagneu-Sotelo
2013   Latino Immigrant Men and the Deportation Crisis: A Gendered Racial Removal Program. *Latino Studies* 11: 271–292.

Gomberg-Muñoz, Ruth
2016   The Juárez Wives Club: Gendered Citizenship and U.S. Immigration Law. *American Ethnologist* 42(2): TBD.
2015   The Punishment/El Castigo: Undocumented Latinos and U.S. Immigration Processing. *Journal of Ethnic and Migration Studies* 41(14): 2235–2252.

2012   Inequality in a "Postracial" Era: Race, Immigration, and Criminalization of Low-Wage Labor. *The DuBois Review* 9(2): 339–353.

2011   *Labor and Legality: An Ethnography of a Mexican Immigrant Network.* New York: Oxford University Press.

Gomberg-Muñoz, Ruth, and Laura Nussbaum-Barberena

2011   Is Immigration Policy Labor Policy?: Immigration Enforcement, Undocumented Labor, and the State. *Human Organization* 70(4): 366–375.

Gonzales, Roberto G.

2011   Learning to Be Illegal: Undocumented Youth and Shifting Legal Contexts in the Transition to Adulthood. *American Sociological Review* 76(4): 602–619.

Gonzales, Roberto G., and Leo R. Chavez

2012   "Awakening to a Nightmare": Abjectivity and Illegality in the Lives of Undocumented 1.5 Generation Latino Immigrants in the United States. *Current Anthropology* 53(3): 255–281.

Gould, Stephen

1981   *The Mismeasure of Man.* New York: Norton.

Greider, William

1997   *One World, Ready or Not: The Manic Logic of Global Capitalism,* 2nd ed. New York: Simon & Schuster.

Guelespe, Diana Maritza

2013   *Second-Class Families: The Challenges and Strategies of Mixed-Status Immigrant Families.* Ph.D. dissertation, Department of Sociology, Loyola University Chicago.

Gutierrez, David G.

1995   *Walls and Mirrors: Mexican Americans, Mexican Immigrants, and the Politics of Ethnicity.* Berkeley: University of California Press.

Hagan, Jacqueline

1994   *Deciding to Be Legal: A Maya Community in Houston.* Philadelphia: Temple University Press.

Hagan, Jacqueline Maria, Nestor Rodriguez, and Brianna Castro

2011   Social Effects of Mass Deportations by the United States Government, 2000–10. *Ethnic and Racial Studies* 34(8): 1374–1391.

Herzfeld, Michael

1992   *The Social Production of Indifference: Exploring the Symbolic Roots of Western Bureaucracy.* Chicago: University of Chicago Press.

Heyman, Josiah McC.

2010   *Human Rights and Social Justice Briefing 1: Arizona's Immigration Law—SB 1070.* Oklahoma City: Society for Applied Anthropology.

2001   Class and Classification at the U.S.–Mexico Border. *Human Organization* 60(2): 128–140.

1998   State Effects on Labor Exploitation: The INS and Undocumented Immigrants at the Mexico–United States Border. *Critique of Anthropology* 18(2): 157–180.

Holmes, Seth

2013   *Fresh Fruit, Broken Bodies: Migrant Farmworkers in the United States.* Berkeley: University of California Press.

Hondagneu-Sotelo, Pierrette

1994   *Gendered Transitions: Mexican Experiences of Immigration.* Berkeley: University of California Press.

Horton, Sarah

2016   *They Leave Their Kidneys in the Fields: Injury, Illness, and Illegality Among U.S. Farmworkers.* Berkeley: University of California Press.

2015   Identity Loan: The Moral Economy of Document Exchange in California's Central Valley. *American Ethnologist* 42(1): 55–67.

2014   Debating "Medical Citizenship": Policies Shaping Immigrants' Learned Avoidance of the US Health Care System. In *Hidden Lives and Human Rights in the United States: Understanding the Controversies and Tragedies in Undocumented Immigration*, edited by Lois A. Lorentzen, vol. 3, pp. 297–320. Santa Barbara, CA: ABC-CLIO.

Human Rights Watch

2013   *Mexico's Disappeared: The Enduring Cost of a Crisis Ignored.* February 20. http://www.hrw.org/reports/2013/02/20/mexicos-disappeared-0/, accessed July 25, 2015.

Huntington, Samuel. 2004. Jose Can You See: On How Hispanic Immigrants Threaten America's Identity. *Foreign Policy* 141: 30–45.

Immigrant Legal Resource Center. 2012. *A Guide for Immigration Advocates: Teaching, Interpreting, and Changing Law since 1979*, 18th ed. San Francisco: Immigrant Legal Resource Center.

James, Frank

2013   *Immigration Overhaul Seems on Track despite Boston Tragedy.* National Public Radio, It's All Politics. http://www.npr.org/sections/itsallpolitics/2013/04/22/178483182/immigration-overhaul-seems-on-track-despite-boston-tragedy/, accessed July 24, 2015.

Jimenez, Maria

2009   *Humanitarian Crisis: Migrant Deaths at the U.S.–Mexico Border.* San Diego: ACLU of San Diego & Imperial Counties and Mexico's National Commission of Human Rights.

Jordan, Miriam

2012   Tattoo Checks Trip Up Visas. *Wall Street Journal*. Politics and Policy
        Section. July 11. http://online.wsj.com/news/articles/SB100014240527023
        0393340457750519226598710O#printMode/, accessed October 22, 2014.

Kanstroom, Daniel

2014   *Aftermath: Deportation Law and the New American Diaspora*. New
        York: Oxford University Press.

Kochhar, Rakesh

2005   *Survey of Mexican Migrants Part Three: The Economic Transition
        to America*. Washington, DC: Pew Hispanic Center. Electronic
        document.

Kohli, Aarti, Peter L. Markowitz, and Lisa Chavez

2011   *Secure Communities by the Numbers: An Analysis of Demographics and
        Due Process*. Research Report. Berkeley: Chief Justice Earl Warren
        Institute on Race, Ethnicity & Diversity Berkeley Law Center for
        Research and Administration. http://www.warreninstitute.org/.

Kowalski, Daniel

2015   *From AILA: USCIS Provides I-601 and I-601A Statistics for FY20110—
        FY20115*. American Immigration Lawyers Association Doc. No.
        15042903. April 29.

Lacayo, A. E.

2010   *The Impact of Section 287(g) of the Immigration and Nationality Act
        on the Latino Community*. National Council of La Raza. http://
        publications.nclr.org/bitstream/handle/123456789/1067/287g_
        issuebrief_pubstore.pdf?sequence=1, accessed October 23, 2014.

Lee, Erica

1999   American Gatekeeping: Race and Immigration Law in the Twentieth
        Century. In *Not Just Black and White: Historical and Contemporary
        Perspectives on Immigration, Race, and Ethnicity in the United States*,
        edited by N. Foner and G. Fredrickson, pp. 119–144. New York: Russell
        Sage Foundation.

Leiden, Warren, and David Neal

1990   Highlights of the U.S. Immigration Act of 1990. *Fordham
        International Law Journal* 14(1): 328–339.

Light, Michael T., Mark Hugo Lopez, and Ana Gonzalez-Barrera

2014   *The Rise of Federal Immigration Crimes: Unlawful Reentry Drives
        Growth*. Washington, DC: Pew Research Center's Hispanic Trends
        Project.

Linker, Jodi
2013   A "S.A.F.E" Approach to Defending Illegal Reentry Cases. Orlando: Winning Strategies Seminar.

Lipman, Francine
2006   The Taxation of Undocumented Immigrants: Separate, Unequal, and without Representation. *Harvard Latino Law Review* 9: 1–58.

Mahler, Sarah J.
1995   *American Dreaming: Immigrant Life on the Margins*. Princeton, NJ: Princeton University Press.

Mahr, J., and R. McCoppin
2009   *Study Suggests Racial Mislabeling Skews McHenry County Sheriff Data*. Chicago Tribune, March 26. http://articles.chicagotribune.com/2011-03-26/news/ct-met-mchenry-profiling-20110326_1_hispanics-mislabeling-deputies, accessed September 28, 2011.

Massey, Douglas
2009   Racial Formation in Theory and Practice: The Case of Mexicans in the United States. *Race and Social Problems* 1: 12–26.

Massey, Douglas, Jorge Durand, and Nolan J. Malone
2002   *Beyond Smoke and Mirrors: Mexican Immigration in an Era of Economic Integration*. New York: Russell Sage Foundation.

McKay, Ramah
2003   *Family Reunification*. Migration Policy Institute, May 3. http://www.migrationpolicy.org/article/family-reunification/, accessed December 10, 2014.

Mehta, Chirag, Nik Theodore, Iliana Mora, and Jennifer Wade
2002   *Chicago's Undocumented Immigrants: An Analysis of Wages, Working Conditions, and Economic Contributions*. Chicago: UIC Center for Urban Economic Development.

Menchaca, Martha, and Richard Valencia
1990   Anglo-Saxon Ideologies in the 1920s–1930s: Their Impact on the Segregation of Mexican Students in California. *Anthropology & Education Quarterly* 21: 222–249.

Menjívar, Cecilia
2006   Liminal Legality: Salvadoran and Guatemalan Immigrants' Lives in the United States. *The American Journal of Sociology* 111(4): 999–1037.

Menjívar, Cecilia, and Daniel Kanstroom
2014   *Constructing Illegality in America: Immigrant Experiences, Critiques, and Resistance*. New York: Cambridge University Press.

Meyers, Deborah
2005   *US Border Enforcement: From Horseback to High-Tech.* Washington, DC: Migration Policy Institute.

Miroff, Nick
2013   *Controversial Quota Drives Immigrant Detention Boom.* The *Washington Post.* October 13. https://www.washingtonpost.com/world/controversial-quota drives-im...-boom/2013/10/13/09bb689e-214c-11e3-ad1a-1a919f2ed890_print.html/, accessed July 24, 2015.

N., Jose Angel
2014   *Illegal: Reflections of an Undocumented Immigrant.* Champaign: University of Illinois Press.

Nakano Glenn, Evelyn
2002   *Unequal Freedom: How Race and Gender Shaped American Citizenship and Labor.* Cambridge, MA: Harvard University Press.

National Conference of State Legislatures
2011   *Immigration-Related Laws and Resolutions in the States (January–June). Immigration Policy Report,* September 19. http://www.ncsl.org/issues-research/immig/state-immigration-laws-january-to-june-2011.aspx/, accessed December 14, 2012.

Ngai, Mae
2004   *Impossible Subjects: Illegal Aliens and the Making of Modern America.* Princeton, NJ: Princeton University Press.

O'Leary, Anna Ochoa, and Azucena Sanchez
2011   Anti-Immigrant Arizona: Ripple Effects and Mixed Immigration Status Households under "Policies of Attrition" Considered. *Journal of Borderlands Studies* 26(1): 115–133.

Pallares, Amalia
2014   *Family Activism: Immigrant Struggle and the Politics of Noncitizenship.* New Brunswick, NJ: Rutgers University Press.

Passel, Jeffrey, and D'Vera Cohn
2009   *A Portrait of Unauthorized Immigrants in the United States.* April 14. Washington, DC: Pew Hispanic Center. http://www.pewhispanic.org/files/reports/107.pdf/, accessed May 22, 2013.

Pedraza, Silvia, and Ruben G. Rumbaut
1996   *Origins and Destinies: Immigration, Race, and Ethnicity in America.* New York: Wadsworth.

Perkinson, Robert
2010   *Texas Tough: The Rise of America's Prison Empire.* New York: Holt.

Pew Hispanic Center
2006   *Fact Sheet: Modes of Entry for the Unauthorized Migrant Population.*
        May 22. http://www.pewhispanic.org/2006/05/22/modes-of-entry-
        for-the-unauthorized-migrant-population/, accessed April 19, 2013.

Plascencia, Luis
2009   The "Undocumented" Mexican Migrant Question: Re-Examining
        the Framing of Law and Illegalization in the United States. *Urban
        Anthropology* 38 (2–4): 376–434.

Portes, Alejandro, and John Walton
1981   *Labor, Class, and the International System.* New York: Academic
        Press.

Powers, Mary, William Seltzer, and Jing Shi
1998   Gender Differences in the Occupational Status of Undocumented
        Immigrants in the United States: Experience before and after
        Legalization. *International Migration Review* 32(4): 1015–1046.

Quesada, James, Sonya Arreola, Alex Kral, Sahar Khoury, Kurt C. Organista,
        and Paula Worby
2014   "As Good as It Gets": Undocumented Latino Day Laborers Negotiating
        Discrimination in San Francisco and Berkeley, California, USA. *City &
        Society* 26(1): 29–50.

Ready, Timothy, and Allert Brown-Gort
2005   *The State of Latino Chicago: This Is Home Now.* Notre Dame: Institute
        for Latino Studies. Electronic document.

Romero, Mary
2008   The Inclusion of Citizenship Status in Intersectionality: What
        Immigration Raids Tell Us about Mixed Status Families, the State and
        Assimilation. *International Journal of Sociology of the Family* 34(2):
        131–152.

Rytina, Nancy
2002   *IRCA Legalization Effects: Lawful Permanent Residence and
        Naturalization through 2001.* Paper presented at the Effects of
        Immigrant Legalization Programs on the United States: Scientific
        Evidence on Immigrant Adaptation and Impacts on U.S. Economy and
        Society, Bethesda, MD, October 25.

Sahlins, Marshall
2013   *What Kinship Is—And Is Not.* Chicago: University of Chicago Press.

Salcido, Olivia, and Madelaine Adelman
2004   "He Has Me Tied with the Blessed and Damned Papers":
       Undocumented-Immigrant Battered Women in Phoenix, Arizona.
       Human Organization 63(2): 162–172.

Salcido, Olivia, and Cecilia Menjívar
2012   Gendered Paths to Legal Citizenship: The Case of Latin American
       Immigrants in Phoenix, Arizona. Law & Society Review 46(2): 335–368.

Sassen-Koob, Saskia
1981   Towards a Conceptualization of Immigrant Labor. Social Problems 29:
       65–85.

Schmalzbauer, Leah
2014   The Last Best Place? Gender, Family, and Migration in the New West.
       Stanford, CA: Stanford University Press.

Schreiber, Susan, and Charles Wheeler
2013   Update from the NBC on Provisional Waivers. CLINIC. https://
       cliniclegal.org/print/8809/, accessed October 23, 2013.

Schuck, Peter
1998   Citizens, Strangers, and In-Betweens: Essays on Immigration and
       Citizenship. Boulder, CO: Westview Press.

Selway, William, and Margaret Newkirk,
2013   Congress Mandates Jail Beds for 34,000 Immigrants as Private Prisons
       Profit. Bloomberg. September 24. http://www.bloomberg.com/
       news/2013-09-24/congress-fuels-private-jails-detaining-34-000-
       immigrants.html/.

Shoichet, Catherine E.
2011   Georgia Governor: Probationers Could Fill Farm Jobs. CNN, June 14.
       http://www.cnn.com/2011/POLITICS/06/14/georgia.farm.workers
       .immigration/index.html/, accessed June 15, 2011.

Stack, Carol
1974   All Our Kin. New York: Basic Books.

Stephen, Lynn
2007   Transborder Lives: Indigenous Oaxacans in Mexico, California, and
       Oregon. Durham, NC: Duke University Press.

Striffler, Steve
2007   Neither Here nor There: Mexican Immigrant Workers and the Search
       for Home. American Ethnologist 34(4): 674–688.

Sullivan, Laura
2010   *Prison Economics Help Drive Arizona Immigration Law.* National Public Radio. Oct 28. http://www.npr.org/templates/story/story .php?storyId=130833741/, accessed July 28, 2015.

Taylor, Paul, Mark Hugo Lopez, Jeffrey Passel, and Seth Motel
2011   *Unauthorized Immigrants: Length of Residency, Patterns of Parenthood.* Washington, DC: Pew Hispanic Center. http://www .pewhispanic.org/2011/12/01/unauthorized-immigrants-length-of-residency-patterns-of-parenthood/, accessed May 22, 2013.

Ticktin, Miriam
2006   Where Ethics and Politics Meet: The Violence of Humanitarianism in France. *American Ethnologist* 33(1): 33–49.

Torres, Maria de los Angeles
2003   *The Lost Apple: Operation Pedro Pan, Cuban Children in the U.S., and the Promise of a Better Future.* Boston: Beacon Press.

Univision.com
2009   *A Falta de Inmigrantes, Reclusos: Escasez de Campesinos en Campos de Idaho.* [*When Immigrants Are Scarce, Prisoners: A Shortage of Farmworkers in the Fields of Idaho.*] http://www.univision.com/ content/content.jhtml?cid=1226109#/, accessed December 31, 2009.

UN Office on Drugs and Crime
2013   *Global Study on Homicide 2013: Trends, Contexts, Data.* Vienna: United Nations publication, Sales No. 14.IV.1

Urbina, Ian
2014   *Using Jailed Migrants as a Pool of Cheap Labor. New York Times.* May 24. http://mobile.nytimes.com/2014/05/25/us/using-jailed-migrants-as-a-pool-of-cheap-labor.html?hp&_r=2&referrer=/, accessed July 20, 2015.

U.S. Customs and Border Protection
2014   *Southwest Border Deaths by Fiscal Year.* Washington, DC: U.S. Border Patrol. https://www.cbp.gov/sites/default/files/documents/BP%20 Southwest%20Border%20Sector%20Deaths%20FY1998%20-%20 FY2014_0.pdf/, accessed July 28, 2015.

U.S. Department of Homeland Security
2013   *Yearbook of Immigration Statistics: 2012.* Washington, DC: U.S. Department of Homeland Security, Office of Immigration Statistics.
2012   *I-601 Waivers of Inadmissibility: Does the Current Process Work? When Is Hardship Extreme? Do Alternative Models Exist?* http://www.dhs

.gov/i-601-waivers-inadmissibility-does-current-process-work-when-hardship-extreme-do-alternative-models/, accessed July 2, 2015.

U.S. Department of State, Bureau of Consular Affairs
2015   DV 2015–Selected Entrants. http://travel.state.gov/content/visas/english/immigrate/diversity-visa/dv-2015-selected-entrants.html/, accessed July 28, 2015.
2014   Visa Waiver Program. http://travel.state.gov/content/visas/english/visit/visa-waiver-program.html/, accessed October 23, 2014.

U.S. Department of State, Bureau of Diplomatic Security
2015   OSAC 2015 Cuba Crime and Safety Report. https://www.osac.gov/pages/ContentReportDetails.aspx?cid=17198/, accessed July 28, 2015.

U.S. Government Accountability Office
2009   Secure Border Initiative Fence Construction Costs. GAO-09-244R. Washington, DC: Government Accountability Office.

U.S. Immigration and Customs Enforcement
2014a   Activated Jurisdictions. http://www.ice.gov/doclib/secure-communities/pdf/sc-activated.pdf/, accessed October 23, 2014.
2014b   Secure Communities: Get the Facts. http://www.ice.gov/secure-communities/get-the-facts/, accessed July 28, 2015.

Valdez, Diana Washington
2014   Dangerous Cities: Juarez Drops in Violence Rank. El Paso Times, January 18. http://www.elpasotimes.com/news/ci_24939627/ju-rez-and-four-u-s-cities-among/, accessed July 28, 2015.

Vargas, Jose Antonio
2012   We Are Americans.* *Just Not Legally. Time Magazine, June 25.

Varsanyi, Monica
2011 Neoliberalism and Nativism: Local Anti-immigrant Policy Activism and an Emerging Politics of Scale. International Journal of Urban and Regional Research 35(2): 295–311.

Watkins, Boyce
2011   Corporations Take Advantage of Prison Labor: Capitalism Leads to Exploitation of Inmates. The Loop 21. http://theloop21.com/money/corporations-take-advantage-prison-labor/, accessed June 3, 2011.

Welna, David
2013   Meet the Virginian Shaping the House GOP's Immigration Plan. National Public Radio. It's All Politics. February 21.

Western, Bruce
2006   Punishment and Inequality in America. New York: Russell Sage Foundation.

Weston, Kath
1997   *Families We Choose: Lesbians, Gays, Kinship*, revised ed. New York: Columbia University Press.

Willen, Sarah
2007   Toward a Critical Phenomenology of "Illegality": State Power, Criminalization, and Abjectivity among Undocumented Workers in Tel Aviv, Israel. *International Migration* 34(3): 8–38.

Yanagisako, Sylvia Junko, and Jane Fishburne Collier
1987   Toward a Unified Analysis of Gender and Kinship. In *Gender and Kinship: Essays toward a Unified Analysis*, edited by Jane Fishburne Collier and Sylvia Junko Yanagisako. Stanford, CA: Stanford University Press.

Zamudio, Maria Ines
2011   The Allure of Secure. *Chicago Reporter*, November 1.

Zavella, Patricia
2011   *I'm Neither Here nor There: Mexicans' Quotidian Struggles with Migration and Poverty*. Durham, NC: Duke University Press.

Zlolniski, Christian
2006   *Janitors, Street Vendors, and Activists: The Lives of Mexican Immigrants in Silicon Valley*. Berkeley: University of California Press.
2003   Labor Control and Resistance of Mexican Immigrant Janitors in Silicon Valley. *Human Organization* 62(1): 39–49.

Zong, Jie, and Jeanne Batalova
2015   *Frequently Requested Statistics on Immigrants and Immigration in the United States*. Washington, DC: Migration Policy Institute. http://www.migrationpolicy.org/article/frequently-requested-statistics-immigrants-and-immigration-united-states/, accessed July 24, 2015.

INDEX

DATE ~~~